Telephone Numbers & Information

Emergency Telephone Numbers

Emergency Medical Service (EMS): _____

Ambulance Service: _____

Fire: _____

Police: _____

Crisis Intervention Center: _____

Suicide Prevention Center: _____

Poison Control Center: _____

Pharmacy: _____

24-Hour Pharmacy: _____

Hospital: _____

Health Care Professionals:

Doctors (family physician, internists, specialists):

Name	Specialty	Telephone Number(s)
_____	_____	_____
_____	_____	_____
_____	_____	_____

Dentist: _____

Employee Assistance Program (EAP): _____

Health Insurance Company Information:

Company Name: _____

Address: _____

Phone Number: _____

Policy Holder's Name: _____

Policy Number: _____

Social Security Number: _____

Medicare Information: _____

    Effective Date: Hospital Insurance: _____

                          Medical Insurance: _____

Medicaid Information: _____

    Effective Date: _____

W9-BVQ-554

NOTICE

This book is not intended as a comprehensive guide to health care, nor should you substitute the information it contains for expert medical advice or treatment. The information is designed to help you make informed choices about your health. If, while under a physician's care, you receive advice that is contrary to this book, follow your doctor's advice instead. If the problem you are reading about doesn't go away after a reasonable amount of time, you should see or call your doctor.

Acknowledgements:

The material in the *HealthyLife® 50-Plus Self-Care Guide* went through an extensive review process in order to ensure medical accuracy and present the latest medical research. We are indebted to the physicians and other health professionals who served on our clinical review team.

Myron Miller, M.D., Vice-Chairman and Professor, Department of Geriatrics and Adult Development, The Mount Sinai School of Medicine, New York, New York

Mark H. Beers, M.D., Senior Director of Geriatrics and Associate Editor, Merck Manual, West Point, Pennsylvania

Edward Adler, M.D., S.A.C.P., Attending Physician, Division of Geriatric Medicine, William Beaumont Hospital, Royal Oak, Michigan; Clinical Assistant Professor of Medicine, Wayne State University School of Medicine, Detroit, Michigan

Joel Schoolin, D.O., Associate Medical Director, Lutheran General Health Plan, Mt. Prospect, Illinois

Don R. Powell, Ph.D., President, American Institute for Preventive Medicine, Farmington Hills, Michigan

Jeanette Karwan, R.D., Director, Product Development, American Institute for Preventive Medicine, Farmington Hills, Michigan

Elaine Frank, M.Ed., R.D., Vice President, American Institute for Preventive Medicine, Farmington Hills, Michigan

Jacquelyn B. Elmers, Manager, Graphic Design, American Institute for Preventive Medicine, Farmington Hills, Michigan

HealthyLife® 50-Plus Self-Care Guide is one of a series of publications and programs offered by the American Institute for Preventive Medicine designed to help individuals improve the quality of their lives. Other self-care guides address the needs of Adults, (also available in Low-Literacy and Spanish editions), Children and Women. For more information, call or write:

American Institute for Preventive Medicine
30445 Northwestern Hwy., Suite 350
Farmington Hills, Michigan 48334
(810) 539-1800 / FAX (810) 539-1808

Table of Contents

Health Problems

Major Medical Conditions

Appendices

Introduction

Now, more than ever, mature adults need to be responsible for their own health care. The emotional and economic costs that come with illness keep going up. Insurance costs have risen for private citizens, employers and the government, (medicare, medicaid). There are increased co-pays and higher deductibles. Lab tests, medicines, and doctor office visits cost more, as well.

Medical care has also become harder to keep up with. You have to make a lot of decisions when you get sick:

☐ Should I go to the emergency room?

☐ Should I call my doctor?

☐ Can I wait and see if it gets better?

☐ Can I take care of it myself?

☐ What should I do?

The *HealthyLife® 50-Plus Self-Care Guide* can help you make these decisions. The guide contains two sections. The first one is about 26 of the most common health problems in people over fifty. It tells you what you can do when you have one of these problems.

Each of these 26 health problems is divided into 3 parts:

☐ Facts about the problem: What it is, what causes it, symptoms and treatments.

☐ YES or NO questions to help you decide if you should seek emergency care, see your doctor, call your doctor or use self-care procedures.

☐ A list of self-care treatments for the problem.

Sometimes you can treat these conditions yourself. Sometimes you need medical help. This section of the *HealthyLife® 50-Plus Self-Care Guide* can help you ask the right questions, find answers and most importantly, protect your most precious resource, your health.

The second section presents 15 major medical conditions that are common to older persons. Each of the conditions are divided into 3 parts:

☐ Information about the condition.

☐ Signs and symptoms of the condition.

☐ Care and treatment for the condition.

Unlike the common health problems in the first section, which may be treated with self-care procedures alone, these 15 medical conditions need a doctor's diagnosis and medical treatment. But, there will still be things you need to do to take care of yourself, if you have one or more of these conditions.

How To Use the Self-Care Section

☐ Locate the health problem you wish to learn more about in the Table of Contents. They are listed alphabetically.

☐ Read the first section which gives general information about the medical condition, what it is, what causes it, if known, and its symptoms and treatments. When possible, preventive measures are identified.

☐ Next, read the "Questions to Ask" section. Answer YES or NO to each question beginning with the first one. Your YES or NO responses will indicate whether you should SEEK EMERGENCY CARE, SEE YOUR DOCTOR, CALL YOUR DOCTOR, or use SELF-CARE PROCEDURES listed at the end of the flow chart.

What the Instructions Mean

 ## Seek Emergency Care

You should get help fast. Go to the hospital emergency room or call for emergency medical service (EMS), from your city EMS department or local ambulance service.

Make sure you know a phone number for emergency medical help. Write it down near your phone and in the "Emergency Phone Numbers" list on page 1 of this book.

 ## See Doctor

The term "Doctor" can be used for a number of health care providers. They include:

- [ ] Your physician.

- [ ] Your Health Maintenance Organization (HMO) clinic, primary doctor or other designated health professional.

- [ ] Walk-in clinic or urgent care center.

- [ ] Physician's assistants (P.A.s), Certified Nurses (C.N.s), who work with your doctor.

- [ ] Home health care provider.

- [ ] Your dentist.

When you see the "See Doctor" symbol, you should do so as soon as you can. You may need medicine or treatment to keep the prob-lem from getting worse. Call first and ask for an appointment or for immediate care. Tell the nurse or receptionist what's wrong if you can't talk to your doctor directly. If you can't be seen soon, ask for a referral. A referral from your doctor can help you get to see someone else who can help you.

 ## Call Doctor

Call your doctor and state the problem. He/she can decide what you should do. He/she may:

- [ ] Tell you to make an appointment to be seen.

- [ ] Send you to a laboratory for tests.

- [ ] Prescribe medicine or treatment over the phone.

- [ ] Give you specific instructions to treat the problem.

 ## Provide Self-Care

You can probably take care of the problem yourself if you answered NO to all the questions. Use the Self-Care Procedures that are listed. But call your doctor if you don't feel better soon. You may have some other problem.

1 Backaches

There are many causes of backaches. These include:

- ☐ Muscular strain of the lower back.

- ☐ Back injury such as a slipped or herniated disk, spinal fracture, etc.

- ☐ Osteoarthritis. (See page 98).

- ☐ Osteoporosis. (See page 114).

- ☐ Urinary tract infection. (See page 85).

- ☐ Acute inflammation of the prostate gland in men, known as prostatitis.

- ☐ Cancer.

The goals of treatment are to:

- ☐ Treat the cause of the backache.

- ☐ Relieve the pain.

- ☐ Promote healing.

- ☐ Avoid re-injury.

Aspirin and other painkillers can relieve back pain but can't correct back problems.

Aspirin or one of the many non-steroidal anti-inflammatory agents, such as ibuprofen and naproxen sodium can reduce swelling and dull the pain. Taking aspirin with antacids or in a buffered form can reduce the stomach upset associated with it. Check with your doctor before taking any of these to make sure you are taking the medicine that is best for you.

Doctors sometimes prescribe stronger pain killers that contain codeine.

Muscle relaxants relieve painful muscle spasms and make it easier to rest in bed. You need a prescription for muscle relaxants. Your doctor may or may not prescribe muscle relaxants. This will depend on your age and other medicines you take.

Prevention

You may prevent back pain caused by muscular strain by using proper lifting techniques.

The Dos and Don'ts of Lifting

It's all too familiar. You go to lift an object of some kind, and out of nowhere, the pain hits. Want to avoid hurting your back? Follow the dos and don'ts of proper lifting.

First, the dos:

- ☐ Wear good support shoes, not sandals or high heels.

7

Backaches, continued

- [ ] Plant your feet squarely and stand close to the object you plan to lift.

- [ ] Bend at the knees, not at the waist. Keep your knees bent as you lift.

- [ ] Keep your back as straight as you can.

- [ ] Pull in your stomach muscles and tuck in your rear end.

- [ ] Let your legs carry the weight.

- [ ] Hold the object very close to your body.

- [ ] Lift slowly.

- [ ] Get help if the object is too heavy or large for one person to handle.

- [ ] Use a dolly or other device to move something heavy.

The don'ts:

- [ ] Don't lift a load that's too heavy.

- [ ] Don't bend at the waist to pick up objects.

- [ ] Don't arch your back when lifting or carrying anything.

- [ ] Don't twist your back when holding an object. Instead, turn your whole body, head to toe, in the direction you're headed.

- [ ] Don't lift heavy things over your head.

- [ ] Don't lift too fast or with a jerk.

- [ ] Don't lift something heavy with one hand and something light in the other. Balance the load.

- [ ] Don't try to lift an object such as a child with one arm while holding on to something else, such as a grocery bag with the other. Put one down or lift both objects at the same time.

- [ ] Don't lift anything heavy if you're not steady on your feet.

- [ ] Don't lift if your feet are too close together. Stand with your feet shoulder-width apart for stability.

- [ ] Don't lift if your back hurts.

- [ ] Don't lift if you have a history of back trouble.

Questions To Ask

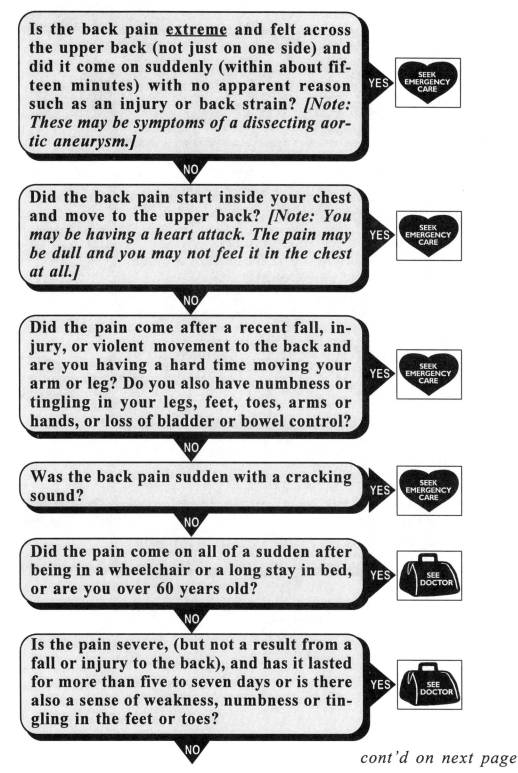

Is the back pain <u>extreme</u> and felt across the upper back (not just on one side) and did it come on suddenly (within about fifteen minutes) with no apparent reason such as an injury or back strain? *[Note: These may be symptoms of a dissecting aortic aneurysm.]*

YES ▶ SEEK EMERGENCY CARE

NO

Did the back pain start inside your chest and move to the upper back? *[Note: You may be having a heart attack. The pain may be dull and you may not feel it in the chest at all.]*

YES ▶ SEEK EMERGENCY CARE

NO

Did the pain come after a recent fall, injury, or violent movement to the back and are you having a hard time moving your arm or leg? Do you also have numbness or tingling in your legs, feet, toes, arms or hands, or loss of bladder or bowel control?

YES ▶ SEEK EMERGENCY CARE

NO

Was the back pain sudden with a cracking sound?

YES ▶ SEEK EMERGENCY CARE

NO

Did the pain come on all of a sudden after being in a wheelchair or a long stay in bed, or are you over 60 years old?

YES ▶ SEE DOCTOR

NO

Is the pain severe, (but not a result from a fall or injury to the back), and has it lasted for more than five to seven days or is there also a sense of weakness, numbness or tingling in the feet or toes?

YES ▶ SEE DOCTOR

NO

cont'd on next page

Backaches, continued

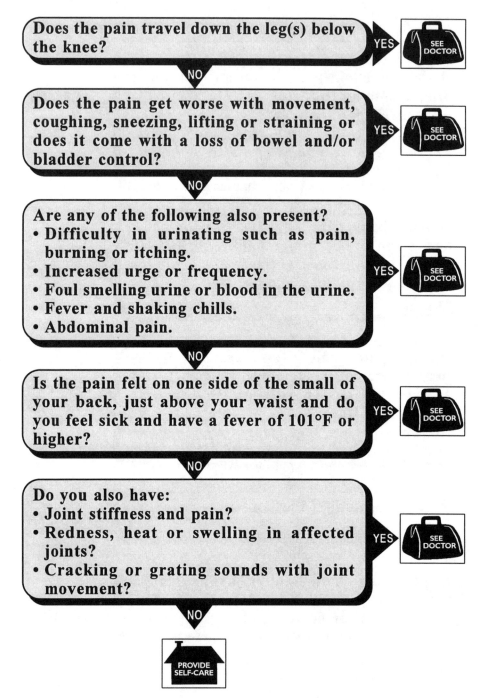

Does the pain travel down the leg(s) below the knee? **YES** → SEE DOCTOR

NO ↓

Does the pain get worse with movement, coughing, sneezing, lifting or straining or does it come with a loss of bowel and/or bladder control? **YES** → SEE DOCTOR

NO ↓

Are any of the following also present?
• Difficulty in urinating such as pain, burning or itching.
• Increased urge or frequency.
• Foul smelling urine or blood in the urine.
• Fever and shaking chills.
• Abdominal pain.
YES → SEE DOCTOR

NO ↓

Is the pain felt on one side of the small of your back, just above your waist and do you feel sick and have a fever of 101°F or higher? **YES** → SEE DOCTOR

NO ↓

Do you also have:
• Joint stiffness and pain?
• Redness, heat or swelling in affected joints?
• Cracking or grating sounds with joint movement?
YES → SEE DOCTOR

NO ↓

PROVIDE SELF-CARE

Backaches, continued

Self-Care Procedures

Bed rest is one of the oldest and best ways to treat back pain. Lying down takes pressure off your back so it can heal faster. Inflammation and swelling go down, too. Two to five days of bed rest is best. Your back muscles can get weak if you stay in bed longer than that. Weak muscles are often what cause backaches in the first place.

To make the most of bed rest:

☐ Only get up when you need to. Move slowly, roll on your side, and swing your legs to the floor. Push off the bed with your arms.

☐ Take pressure off your lower back. Put a pillow under your knees or lie on your side with your knees bent.

☐ Get comfortable when you are lying, standing, and sitting. For example, lie on your back with your knees up. Keep your feet flat on the bed. Tip your hips down and up until you find the best spot.

Cold Treatment

Cold helps with bruises and swelling. You can make a cold pack by wrapping ice in a towel. Use the cold pack for 20 minutes, then take it off for 20 minutes. Do this over and over for 2 to 3 hours a day. Lie on your back with your knees bent, and put the ice pack under your lower back. Start as soon as you hurt your back. Keep doing it for 3 to 4 days.

Heat Treatment

Heat makes blood flow, which helps healing. But don't use heat on a back strain until 3 to 4 days after you get hurt. If you use heat sooner, it can make the pain and swelling worse.

Use a moist heating pad, a hot-water bottle, hot compresses, a hot tub, hot baths, or hot showers. Use heat for 20 minutes, then take the heat off for 20 minutes. Do this up to 3 hours a day. Be careful not to burn yourself.

Massage

Massage won't cure a backache, but it can loosen tight muscles.

Braces or Corsets

Braces and corsets support your back and keep you from moving it too much. They do what strong back muscles do, but they won't make your back stronger.

Relieve the Pain

Take aspirin, ibuprofen, or naproxen sodium for pain. *[Note: Check with your doctor before taking over-the-counter pain medicines, to make sure you take the ones that are best for you.]*

Backaches, continued

Acetaminophen will help with pain, but not swelling.

Don't "overdo it" after taking a pain killer. You can hurt your back more, and then it will take longer to heal.

More Tips

❑ Exercise your stomach and back muscles to make them stronger. Do this after your back heals. Exercise in the morning and afternoon. Always ask your doctor's permission before starting an exercise program.

❑ Don't sit in one place longer than you need to. It strains your lower back.

❑ Sleep on a hard mattress. Never sleep on your stomach. Sleep on your back or side, with your knees bent.

② Breast Lumps, Cancer & Self-Exam

Breast Lumps

Feeling a lump or lumps in your breast(s) can be scary. For a lot of women, the first thought is cancer. The good news is that most breast lumps, 80-90%, are not cancerous. They are usually benign tumors or cysts that do not invade and destroy body tissue or spread to other parts of the body. They can, though, interfere with body functions and may need to be removed. Examples of these breast lumps are:

☐ Cysts (sometimes called fibrocystic breast disease):

- Are fluid filled sacs.

- Are painful and feel lumpy or tender, especially during the week before a menstrual period.

- Can occur near the surface of the skin of the breast and/or be deep within the breast. This second type may need to be tested with a biopsy to make sure it is benign. Also, they may be linked with a higher risk for breast cancer due to their link with hormones made by the ovaries during childbearing years.

☐ Nipple-duct tumors:

- Occur within the part of the nipple that milk flows through.

- Cause a discharge from the nipple.

- Should be surgically removed.

[Note: In rare instances, there can be a bloody discharge from the nipple which could indicate cancer.]

Breast lumps that are benign may go away after menopause.

Tests can be done to tell whether or not a breast lump is benign:

Ultrasound - to tell whether the lump is hollow, which is usually harmless, or if it is solid.

Needle aspiration - a needle is put into the lump to remove fluid.

Biopsy - a sample of breast tissue is taken and examined.

Mammogram - X-ray of breasts to detect breast abnormalities.

Breast Cancer

Breast cancer is the most common form of cancer among women, accounting for 30% of cancers women get. Each year, there are approximately 180,000 new cases of breast cancer and 45,000 deaths from it. Only lung cancer causes more cancer deaths among women.

Breast Lumps, Cancer & Self-Exam, continued

The chance of breast cancer increases dramatically with age. The National Cancer Institute (NCI) has given the following statistics for a woman's chances of developing breast cancer:

By Age	
25	1 in 19,608
30	1 in 2,525
35	1 in 622
40	1 in 217
45	1 in 93
50	1 in 50
55	1 in 33
60	1 in 24
65	1 in 17
70	1 in 14
75	1 in 11
80	1 in 10
85	1 in 9
Ever	1 in 8

Men can also develop breast cancer, but it is very unusual. About 300 men die each year from the disease.

Breast cancer results from malignant tumors that invade and destroy normal tissue.

When these tumors break away and spread to other parts of the body, it is called metastasis. Breast cancer can spread to the lymph nodes, lungs, liver, bone and brain. Breast cancer risks include:

☐ Having had cancer in one breast increases the risk for cancer in the other breast.

☐ Family history of breast cancer, especially for mothers, daughters and sisters of women with breast cancer.

☐ Never giving birth or giving birth after age 30.

☐ Early onset of menstruation (before age 12).

☐ Late menopause (after age 55).

☐ Older than age 40, but especially older than 50.

☐ Exposure to radiation.

☐ Diet high in fat.

☐ Obesity.

☐ Diabetes.

Detection

To detect breast cancer, the American Cancer Society suggests:

☐ Women over age 20 should examine their breasts once a month. (See following section on "Breast Self-Exam".)

☐ Breast self-exam should be done 7-10 days after the start of the menstrual period.

☐ After menopause, women can perform breast self-exam any time of the month, but on the same day each month.

Breast Lumps, Cancer, & Self-Exam, continued

☐ Women with no symptoms of breast cancer should have a mammogram between the ages of 35-39. This would be used as a base line mammogram which could be compared to mammograms taken later in life.

☐ Women aged 40-49 should have a mammogram every one or two years.

☐ Women over age 50 should have a mammogram every year.

[Note: Recommendations for mammograms vary among government and health organizations. Most favor screening early and often. All suggest a mammogram every year or at least every two years after age 50. Any women who notices a lump in her breast or any of the other symptoms mentioned above should see her doctor as soon as possible. Tests can be done to tell if cancerous cells are present.]

Treatment

There are a variety of treatments for breast cancer. The main treatment is surgery. The removal of the cancerous area is most often recommended along with taking a sample of the lymph nodes in the armpit to see if the cancer has spread there.

Other treatments include radiation therapy, chemotherapy and hormonal therapy.

It is important to find out the type of cancer cell that is involved. If the cancer is a type which spreads quickly, a more extensive surgical treatment may be chosen.

Types of Surgical Procedures:

Lumpectomy - the lump and a border of surrounding tissue are removed.

Partial or segmental mastectomy - the tumor and up to one quarter of the breast tissue are removed.

Simple or total mastectomy - the entire breast is removed.

Modified radial mastectomy - the entire breast, the underarm lymph nodes and the lining covering the chest muscles, but not the muscles themselves are removed.

Radical mastectomy - the breast, lymph nodes in the armpit and the chest muscles under the breast are removed.

Ask your doctor about the benefits and risks for each surgical option and decide together which option is best for you.

Breast Lumps, Cancer &
Self-Exam, continued

Questions to Ask

Do you see or feel any lumps, thickening or changes of any kind when you examine your breasts? For example, is there dimpling, puckering, retraction of the skin or change in the shape or contour of the breast? **YES**

NO

Do you have breast pain or a constant tenderness that lasts throughout the menstrual cycle? **YES**

NO

If you normally have lumpy breasts (already diagnosed as being benign by your doctor), do you notice any new lumps or have any lumps changed in size or are you concerned about having "benign" lumps? **YES**

NO

Do the nipples become drawn into the chest or inverted totally, change shape or become crusty from a discharge? **YES**

NO

Is there any discharge when you squeeze the nipple of either breast or both breasts? **YES**

NO

Do you have a family history of breast cancer which leads you to be concerned even if you don't notice any problems when you examine your breasts? **YES**

NO

Continue to Perform Breast Self-Exam Monthly and Use Self-Care and Prevention Procedures.

16

Breast Lumps, Cancer & Self-Exam, continued

Breast Self-Exam

It is normal to have some lumpiness or thickening in the breasts. By examining your breasts once each month, you will learn what is normal for you and when any changes do occur.

How to Examine Your Breasts

 **In the shower** - With your fingers flat, move gently over every part of each breast. Use your right hand to examine the left breast and your left hand to examine the right breast. Check for any thickening, hard lump or knot.

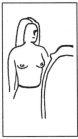 **In front of a mirror** - Check your breasts with your arms at your sides. Then raise your  arms overhead. Look for any changes in the shape of each breast, swelling, dimpling or changes in the nipples.

 **Lying down** - To examine your right breast, put a pillow under your right shoulder. Place your right hand behind your head. Then with the flat fingers of your left hand, press gently in small circular motions around an imaginary nary clock face. Begin at the outermost top of your right breast for 12 o'clock, then move to 10 o'clock, etc. until you get back to 12 o'clock. Each breast will have a normal ridge of firm tissue. Then move in one inch toward the nipple. Keep circling to examine every part of your breast including the nipple. Repeat the procedure on the left breast with a pillow under the left shoulder and your left hand behind your head. Finally, squeeze the nipple of each breast gently between the thumb and index finger. Any discharge, clear or bloody, should be reported to your physician immediately.

Self-Care/Prevention Procedures

For Cystic Breasts:

- ☐ Avoid caffeine in: Beverages (coffee, colas and drinks with chocolate); foods (chocolate); and medicines (appetite suppressants, some pain relievers such as Extra Strength Excedrin, etc.

- ☐ Exercise regularly. This can stimulate circulation to your breasts.

- ☐ Maintain a healthy body weight.

- ☐ Eat a low fat diet. If possible, less than 25% of total calories as fat.

Breast Lumps, Cancer & Self-Exam, continued

☐ Limit salt and sodium intake to prevent fluid buildup in the breasts.

☐ Don't smoke and don't use nicotine gum or patches.

☐ Take pain relievers such as aspirin, acetaminophen, ibuprofen or naproxen sodium.

☐ Wear a bra that provides good support. You may want to wear it while you sleep, too.

☐ For severe discomfort, apply ice packs to your breasts two to three times a day.

☐ Take vitamin E (400 international units (IU) per day).

For Breast Cancer:

☐ Eat a low fat diet, 25% or less of total calories. Focus on fresh fruits and vegetables, whole grains, etc.

☐ Eat vegetables that contain a substance called sulforaphane which may help protect against breast cancer. Examples: Broccoli, cabbage, cauliflower and brussels sprouts.

☐ Avoid unnecessary X-rays. Wear a lead apron when you get dental X-rays and other X-rays not of the chest.

☐ Don't smoke or stop smoking if you do.

☐ Limit foods that are salt-cured, smoked and preserved with nitrites and nitrates. Examples: Hot dogs, bacon, smoked sausage and ham.

☐ Limit alcohol consumption.

③ Chest Pain

Chest pain can be a warning sign for many things. It is most often associated with a heart attack. It can also result from lung problems including pneumonia, bronchitis and lung injuries. A hiatal hernia, heartburn, shingles, pulled muscle and even swallowing too much air (aerophagia), can cause chest pain. It is not always easy to know whether or not to seek medical treatment for chest pain. Generally speaking, when in doubt, check it out. Prompt medical treatment for a heart attack or severe lung injury could be life saving.

Questions to Ask

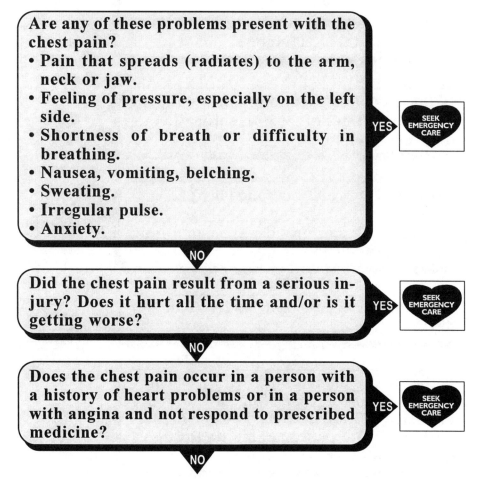

Are any of these problems present with the chest pain?
- Pain that spreads (radiates) to the arm, neck or jaw.
- Feeling of pressure, especially on the left side.
- Shortness of breath or difficulty in breathing.
- Nausea, vomiting, belching.
- Sweating.
- Irregular pulse.
- Anxiety.

YES → SEEK EMERGENCY CARE

NO

Did the chest pain result from a serious injury? Does it hurt all the time and/or is it getting worse?

YES → SEEK EMERGENCY CARE

NO

Does the chest pain occur in a person with a history of heart problems or in a person with angina and not respond to prescribed medicine?

YES → SEEK EMERGENCY CARE

NO

cont'd on next pag

Chest Pain, continued

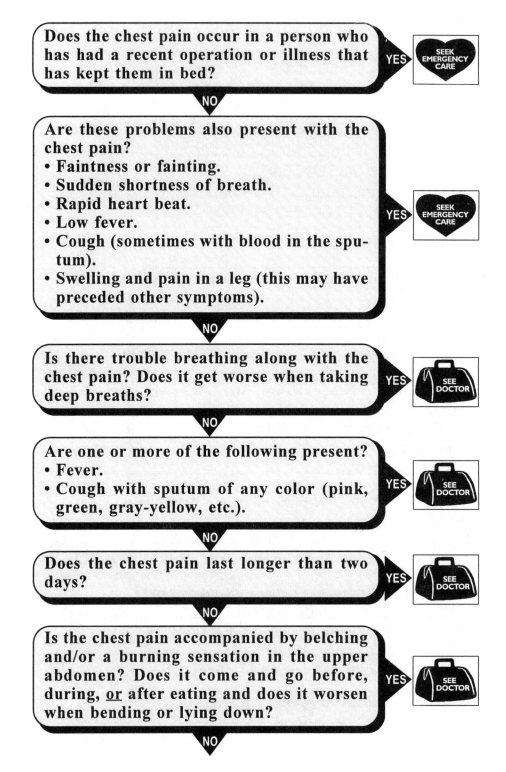

Does the chest pain occur in a person who has had a recent operation or illness that has kept them in bed?

YES → SEEK EMERGENCY CARE

NO ↓

Are these problems also present with the chest pain?
- Faintness or fainting.
- Sudden shortness of breath.
- Rapid heart beat.
- Low fever.
- Cough (sometimes with blood in the sputum).
- Swelling and pain in a leg (this may have preceded other symptoms).

YES → SEEK EMERGENCY CARE

NO ↓

Is there trouble breathing along with the chest pain? Does it get worse when taking deep breaths?

YES → SEE DOCTOR

NO ↓

Are one or more of the following present?
- Fever.
- Cough with sputum of any color (pink, green, gray-yellow, etc.).

YES → SEE DOCTOR

NO ↓

Does the chest pain last longer than two days?

YES → SEE DOCTOR

NO ↓

Is the chest pain accompanied by belching and/or a burning sensation in the upper abdomen? Does it come and go before, during, <u>or</u> after eating and does it worsen when bending or lying down?

YES → SEE DOCTOR

NO ↓

cont'd on next page

Chest Pain, continued

Is the chest pain:
- **Only on one side of the chest?**
- **Not affected by breathing?**
- **Present with a burning feeling and a skin rash at the pain site?**

YES ► SEE DOCTOR

NO

PROVIDE SELF-CARE

Self-Care Procedures:

Self-care procedures for chest pain that results from a pulled muscle or minor injury to the rib cage:

☐ Do not strain the muscle or ribs while pain is felt.

☐ Rest.

☐ Take the pain reliever that your doctor prefers you use, such as aspirin, acetaminophen, ibuprofen or naproxen sodium.

Do call your doctor, though, if the pain lasts longer than two days.

Self-care procedures for chest pain felt with a hiatal hernia:

☐ Lose weight if you are overweight.

☐ Eat 5 or 6 small meals a day instead of 3 meals a day. Do not eat large meals.

☐ Avoid tobacco, alcohol, coffee, spicy and greasy foods.

☐ Take antacids as directed by your doctor, if you have heartburn (and before going to bed).

☐ Don't eat food or drink milk two hours before going to bed.

☐ Don't bend over or lie down after eating.

☐ Don't wear tight clothes, tight belts, or girdles.

☐ Raise the head of your bed by about 3 to 4 inches with blocks (not pillows) when you sleep.

Self-care procedures for chest pain that results from anxiety and hyperventilation:

☐ Try to stay away from people and things that upset you.

☐ Talk about your anxieties with family, friends, or clergy. You may want to see a counselor or psychiatrist if this doesn't help.

☐ Don't take too much aspirin or other drugs that have salicylates.

☐ If you hyperventilate, try this: Cover your mouth and nose with a paper bag and breathe in and out at least 10 times. Take the bag away and try breathing normally. Repeat breathing in and out of the bag if you need to.

❹ Cold Hands & Feet

Many adults 50 and older complain of cold hands and feet. Frequently, the cause is unknown and not serious. Some things known to result in cold hands and feet are:

▢ Poor circulation due to diseased arteries (vessels that carry blood from the heart to the tissues).

▢ Raynaud's disease (disorder that affects the flow of blood to the fingers and sometimes to the toes).

▢ Frostbite.

▢ A side effect of taking certain medications.

▢ Any underlying disease that affects the blood flow in the tiny blood vessels of the skin. Women smokers may be more prone to this last condition.

▢ Stress.

▢ Cervical rib syndrome (compression of the nerves and blood vessels in the neck that affects the shoulders, arms and hands).

Symptoms to be on the lookout for are:

▢ Fingers or toes that turn pale white or blue, then red, in response to cold temperatures.

▢ Pain during the white phase of discoloration.

▢ Tingling or numbness.

Questions to Ask

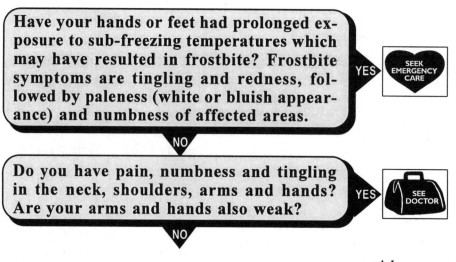

Have your hands or feet had prolonged exposure to sub-freezing temperatures which may have resulted in frostbite? Frostbite symptoms are tingling and redness, followed by paleness (white or bluish appearance) and numbness of affected areas. **YES** → SEEK EMERGENCY CARE

NO ↓

Do you have pain, numbness and tingling in the neck, shoulders, arms and hands? Are your arms and hands also weak? **YES** → SEE DOCTOR

NO ↓

cont'd on next page

Cold Hands & Feet, continued

When exposed to the cold or when you are under stress do your hands or feet:
• Turn pale, then blue then red?
• Get painful and numb?

YES  CALL DOCTOR

NO PROVIDE SELF-CARE

Self-Care Procedures

☐ Wear gloves and wool socks and stay indoors where it's warm.

☐ Don't smoke. It impairs circulation.

☐ Avoid caffeine. It constricts blood vessels.

☐ Avoid handling cold objects. Use ice tongs to pick up ice cubes, for instance.

☐ Stretch your fingers straight out. Swing your arms in large circles, like a baseball pitcher warming up for a game. This may increase blood flow to the fingers. Skip this tip if you have bursitis or back problems.

☐ Do not wear footwear that is tight-fitting.

☐ Wiggle your toes. It may help keep them warm by increasing blood flow.

☐ Practice a relaxation technique such as biofeedback.

⑤ Common Cold

While you read this, approximately 30 million Americans are coughing, sneezing, and blowing their noses. What's wrong with all these people? They've got the most common illness known, the common cold. The average person gets 3 or 4 colds a year. And if you're feeling lucky because you don't have a cold right now, the odds are three out of four that you'll get one during the coming year.

Colds are caused by many different viruses. You can develop an immunity to one type of cold virus, but it won't keep you from getting others. More are lurking everywhere. That's part of the reason we get colds so often.

You know the things that come with a cold:

- ☐ Sneezing.
- ☐ Runny nose.
- ☐ Fever less than 101°F.
- ☐ Sore throat.
- ☐ Dry cough.
- ☐ A cold usually lasts 3 to 7 days, but in older persons, complete recovery may take longer.

How do we get colds? Colds travel from one person to another through coughs and sneezes. But you are more likely to get a cold from mucus on a person's hands when they have a cold. You can pick up the viruses on towels or money. Then someone else picks it up from you. It goes on and on.

Prevention

To lower the risk for catching a cold:

- ☐ Wash your hands often. Keep them away from your nose, eyes, and mouth.
- ☐ Try not to touch people or their things when they have a cold, especially the first 2-4 days they have the cold. This is the most contagious stage.
- ☐ Get lots of exercise. Eat and sleep well.
- ☐ Use a handkerchief or tissues when you sneeze, cough, or blow your nose. This helps keep you from passing viruses to others.

Questions to Ask

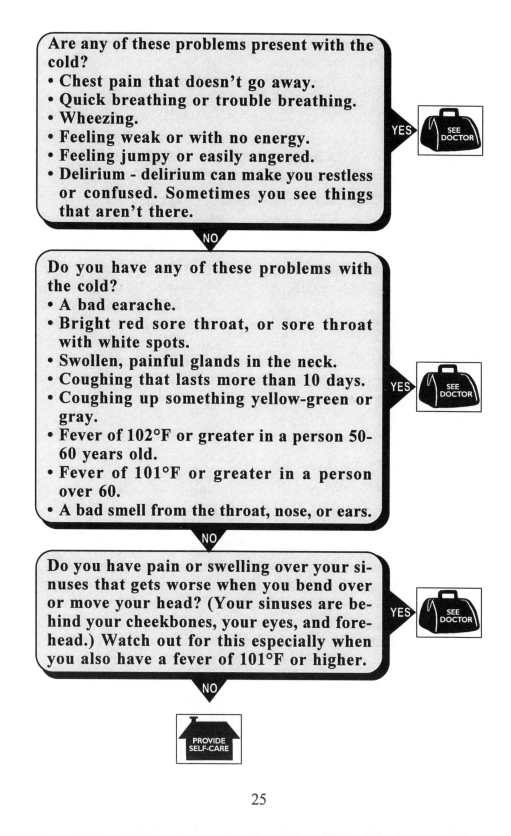

Are any of these problems present with the cold?
- Chest pain that doesn't go away.
- Quick breathing or trouble breathing.
- Wheezing.
- Feeling weak or with no energy.
- Feeling jumpy or easily angered.
- Delirium - delirium can make you restless or confused. Sometimes you see things that aren't there.

YES → SEE DOCTOR

NO ↓

Do you have any of these problems with the cold?
- A bad earache.
- Bright red sore throat, or sore throat with white spots.
- Swollen, painful glands in the neck.
- Coughing that lasts more than 10 days.
- Coughing up something yellow-green or gray.
- Fever of 102°F or greater in a person 50-60 years old.
- Fever of 101°F or greater in a person over 60.
- A bad smell from the throat, nose, or ears.

YES → SEE DOCTOR

NO ↓

Do you have pain or swelling over your sinuses that gets worse when you bend over or move your head? (Your sinuses are behind your cheekbones, your eyes, and forehead.) Watch out for this especially when you also have a fever of 101°F or higher.

YES → SEE DOCTOR

NO ↓

PROVIDE SELF-CARE

Common Cold, continued

Self-Care Procedures

Time is the only cure for a cold. Some things can make you feel better, though. Here are some hints for fighting a cold:

- [ ] Rest in bed if you have a fever.

- [ ] Drink lots of hot or cold drinks. They help clear out your respiratory tract. This can help prevent other problems, like bronchitis.

- [ ] Take aspirin, acetaminophen, ibuprofen or naproxen sodium for muscle aches and pains. *[Note: Take what your doctor prefers you to use.]*

- [ ] Use salt water drops to relieve nasal congestion. Mix ½ teaspoon of salt in 1 cup of warm water. Place in a clean container. Put 3 to 4 drops into each nostril several times a day, with a clean medicine dropper.

- [ ] Gargle with warm salt water, drink tea with honey and lemon or suck on cough drops for a sore throat.

- [ ] Eat chicken soup. (Regular or reduced sodium, if you are on a sodium-restricted diet). It helps clear out mucus.

- [ ] Try taking vitamin C. Even though it has never been medically proven, vitamin C seems to make some people feel better when they have a cold and may help keep them from getting a cold. Consult your doctor about taking vitamin C.

⑥ Constipation

Constipation is when you have trouble having bowel movements. Abdominal swelling, straining during bowel movements, hard stools and the feeling of continued fullness even after a bowel movement are also signs of constipation. It can be very uncomfortable, but it usually doesn't signal disease or a serious problem. What things cause or lead to constipation? A number of things do. These include:

☐ Not drinking enough fluids.

☐ Not eating enough dietary fiber.

☐ Not being active enough.

☐ Using laxatives over a long period of time.

☐ Taking certain medicines (Examples: some heart, pain and anti-depressant medicines as well as antacids, antihistamines, water pills and narcotics).

☐ Not going to the bathroom when you have the urge to have a bowel movement.

In persons fifty and older, the digestive system gets more sluggish. The abdominal and pelvic floor muscles become weaker. These, too, can contribute to constipation.

It is important to know that it is not necessary to have a bowel movement daily. What is more important is what is normal for you.

The "cure" for constipation generally consists of correcting the things that make bowel habits irregular. (See Self-Care Procedures on page 28). You may also need to discuss measures with your doctor about medications and health conditions that could be causing you to be constipated.

Questions To Ask

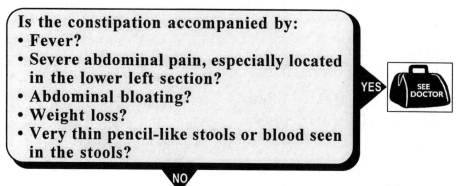

Is the constipation accompanied by:
- **Fever?**
- **Severe abdominal pain, especially located in the lower left section?**
- **Abdominal bloating?**
- **Weight loss?**
- **Very thin pencil-like stools or blood seen in the stools?**

YES → SEE DOCTOR

NO

cont'd on next page

Constipation, continued

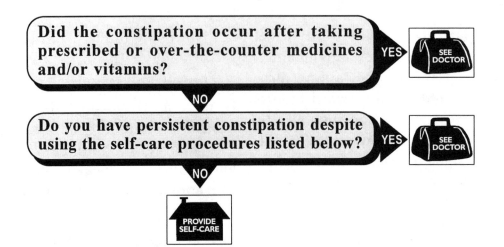

Did the constipation occur after taking prescribed or over-the-counter medicines and/or vitamins? **YES** → SEE DOCTOR

NO

Do you have persistent constipation despite using the self-care procedures listed below? **YES** → SEE DOCTOR

NO

PROVIDE SELF-CARE

Self-Care Procedures

☐ Eat whole-grain breads and cereals and plenty of fresh fruits and vegetables daily. They serve as natural stool softeners thanks in part to their fiber content. One type of fiber from these foods absorbs water like a sponge, turning hard stools into large, soft, easy-to-pass masses.

☐ Drink at least 1½ to 2 quarts of water and other liquids every day.

☐ Drink hot water, tea or coffee. These may help stimulate the bowel.

☐ Get plenty of exercise, to help your bowels move things along.

☐ Don't resist the urge to eliminate or put off a trip to the bathroom.

☐ Keep in mind that drugs such as antacids and iron supplements can be binding, and stay away from them if you get constipated easily. Discuss this with your doctor first.

☐ If necessary, for occasional constipation, you may need an over-the-counter stool softener, mild laxative or enema. Check with your doctor ahead of time so you'll know what is best for you to take if and when you do get constipated.

Ask your doctor about the use of "bulk-forming" laxatives such as Metamucil, Perdiem or Fiber Con. You may be able to use these daily, if necessary. Start out slowly and gradually increase how much you take. Also drink plenty of liquids with them. Bloating, cramping or gas may be noticed at first, but these symptoms should go away in a few weeks or less.

Constipation, continued

Do not use "stimulant" laxatives such as Ex-Lax, Dulcolax, Senokot or enemas without your doctor's permission. Short-term use of them may be O.K., but in the long run, they can make you even more constipated, because your intestines can become lazy and may not work as well on their own. Long term use of these laxatives can also lead to a mineral imbalance, make it harder for your body to benefit from medicines, and lower the amount of nutrients you absorb.

7 Coughs

A lot of things can make you cough. These include: a virus, a bacterial infection, an allergy, cigarette smoke, a foreign object that becomes lodged in the windpipe, and even dry air. Coughing can be a symptom of many diseases as well. Some of these are congestive heart failure, emphysema, lung cancer and tuberculosis. Even certain medicines such as Captopril and Enalapril, which are sometimes used to treat high blood pressure and heart failure, can result in a dry, ticklish cough.

Coughing is a way that your body tries to clear the airways and lungs. Coughing itself is not the problem. What *causes* the cough is the problem? There are 3 kinds of coughs:

Productive - ones that produce mucus or phlegm. You should not try to suppress this type of cough. The cough helps to clear mucus from the lungs.

Non-productive - a dry cough which produces no mucus. This type of cough may come toward the end of a cold or from exposure to smoke or other irritants including dust.

Reflex - a cough which results from an irritation that occurs outside of the respiratory tract such as in the ear or stomach.

Treatment for a cough depends on its type, cause, and the other symptoms that go with it. The focus is to treat the cause and soothe the irritation.

Smoking and second hand smoke should be avoided regardless of the cause of a cough. Smoke causes lung irritation and makes it harder for the body to fight infection.

Questions to Ask

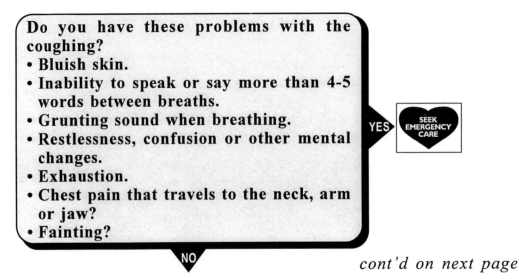

Do you have these problems with the coughing?
- Bluish skin.
- Inability to speak or say more than 4-5 words between breaths.
- Grunting sound when breathing.
- Restlessness, confusion or other mental changes.
- Exhaustion.
- Chest pain that travels to the neck, arm or jaw?
- Fainting?

YES ▶ SEEK EMERGENCY CARE

NO

cont'd on next page

Coughs, continued

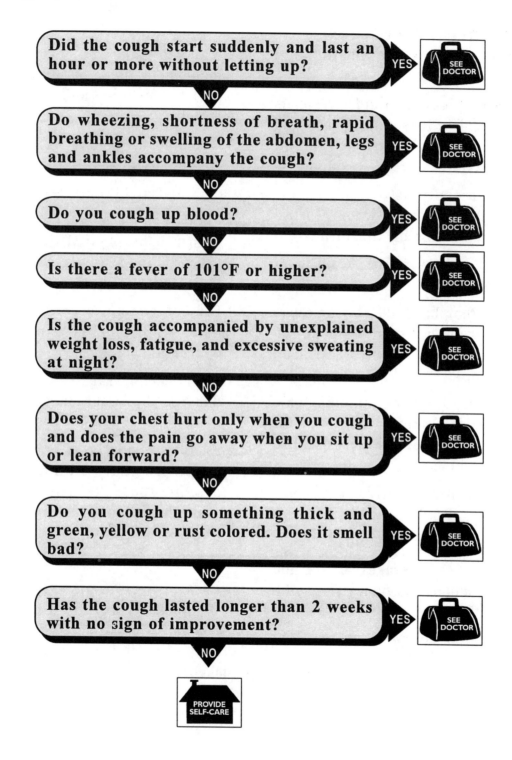

Did the cough start suddenly and last an hour or more without letting up?
YES → SEE DOCTOR
NO ↓

Do wheezing, shortness of breath, rapid breathing or swelling of the abdomen, legs and ankles accompany the cough?
YES → SEE DOCTOR
NO ↓

Do you cough up blood?
YES → SEE DOCTOR
NO ↓

Is there a fever of 101°F or higher?
YES → SEE DOCTOR
NO ↓

Is the cough accompanied by unexplained weight loss, fatigue, and excessive sweating at night?
YES → SEE DOCTOR
NO ↓

Does your chest hurt only when you cough and does the pain go away when you sit up or lean forward?
YES → SEE DOCTOR
NO ↓

Do you cough up something thick and green, yellow or rust colored. Does it smell bad?
YES → SEE DOCTOR
NO ↓

Has the cough lasted longer than 2 weeks with no sign of improvement?
YES → SEE DOCTOR
NO ↓

PROVIDE SELF-CARE

Coughs, continued

Self-Care Procedures

To ease productive (mucus forming) coughs:

- ☐ Drink plenty of fluids. Water is helpful in loosening mucus and also soothes an irritated throat. Fruit juices are also good.

- ☐ Use a cool-mist humidifier especially in the bedroom. Install a humidifier on the furnace.

- ☐ Take a shower. The steam itself may help to thin the mucus.

- ☐ Ask the pharmacist for an over-the-counter expectorant cough preparation.* Robitussin is an example.

- ☐ Stop all forms of smoking. This includes cigarettes, cigars, pipes. Avoid places where smoking takes place.

To ease non-productive (dry, non-mucus forming) coughs:

- ☐ Drink plenty of fluids.

- ☐ Drink hot beverages such as tea with lemon and honey to soothe the throat.

- ☐ Suck on cough drops or hard candy to soothe and moisten the throat.

- ☐ Take an over-the-counter cough suppressant medicine that contains dextromethorphan.* Robitussin-DM is an example.

- ☐ You can make your own cough medicine at home by mixing one part lemon juice and two parts honey.

- ☐ Decongestants may be helpful if there is post-nasal drip.*

Other Self-Care Procedures:

- ☐ Food such as peanuts and popcorn can be inhaled. Eat these types of food slowly and chew them thoroughly.

- ☐ Do not smoke. Avoid second hand smoke. This cannot be overemphasized!

- ☐ Avoid chemical fumes that could damage the lungs causing you to cough.

- ☐ Exercise regularly. A graded exercise program will strengthen breathing muscles and improve your chances of fighting infections.

- ☐ Have your home checked for radon.

* Do check with your doctor or pharmacist to make sure any over-the-counter medicine you select can be taken safely with other medicines you take.

8 Depression

Depression is a condition marked by sadness, hopelessness, helplessness, pessimism, and a lost of interest in life.

A lot of things can lead to depression in persons over 50 years of age:

- ☐ Death or loss of a loved one, or fear of death for oneself.

- ☐ Loss of or a feeling of failure in one's job, marriage or other relationship.

- ☐ Major or chronic illnesses or surgery.

- ☐ Disability.

- ☐ A life change (Examples: A new job, move to a new area, menopause, children grown and have left home, or retirement).

- ☐ Some medicines including certain ones for high blood pressure.

- ☐ Alcohol and/or drug abuse.

- ☐ Hormonal abnormalities.

- ☐ Isolation from others or being in a nursing home.

Even the lack of natural, unfiltered sunlight between late fall and spring can lead to depression in some people. This is called Seasonal Affective Disorder (SAD).

Depression can also be a disease in and of itself caused by brain chemical imbalances.

Symptoms of depression:

- ☐ Persistent feelings of sadness or emptiness.

- ☐ Feelings of helplessness, hopelessness, guilt, and worthlessness.

- ☐ Loss of interest in pleasurable activities, including sex.

- ☐ Sleep disturbances.

- ☐ Fatigue.

- ☐ Loss of energy or enthusiasm.

- ☐ Difficulty in concentrating or making decisions.

- ☐ Ongoing physical symptoms, such as headaches or digestive disorders, that don't respond to treatment.

- ☐ Crying, tearfulness.

- ☐ Poor appetite with weight loss or overeating and weight gain.

In older persons, these usual symptoms of depression may be replaced by such things as dizziness, confusion, refusal to eat or drink, paranoia and what seems to be a loss of mental status.

Whatever the cause, depression can be treated. Treatment includes medicines, psychotherapy, and other therapies that are specific to the cause of the depression such as exposure to bright lights (similar to sunlight) for depression that results from SAD.

Depression, continued
Questions to Ask

Do you have recurrent thoughts of suicide or death? Are you planning ways to commit suicide? **YES**

NO

Have you had markedly diminished interest or pleasure in almost all activities most of the day, nearly every day for at least two weeks or have you been in a depressed mood most of the day, nearly every day for at least two weeks and had any four of the following for at least two weeks?
- Feeling slowed down or restless and unable to sit still.
- Feeling worthless or guilty.
- Changes in appetite or weight loss or gain.
- Thoughts of death or suicide.
- Problems concentrating, thinking, remembering, or making decisions.
- Trouble sleeping or sleeping too much.
- Loss of energy or feeling tired all of the time.
- Headaches.
- Other aches and pains.
- Digestive problems.
- Sexual problems.
- Feeling pessimistic or hopeless.
- Being anxious or worried.

YES

NO

Has the depression appeared after taking over-the-counter or prescription medicine? Is the depression associated with dark, cloudy weather, or winter months, and does it lift when spring comes? **YES**

NO

Depression, continued

Self-Care Procedures

To overcome mild, hard-to-explain depression:

- [ ] Substitute a positive thought for every negative thought that pops into your head.

- [ ] Associate with friendly, positive people. They'll lift your morale.

- [ ] Join a social group, take a class, or get involved in a senior center.

- [ ] Focus your attention away from yourself. Do something to help someone else.

- [ ] Get some physical exercise everyday, even if it's just taking the dog for a walk. Join a mall-walking program with others. If you can do something more exhilarating, like biking, playing tennis or golfing, that's even better.

- [ ] Do something different. Walk or drive to someplace new, or try a new restaurant.

- [ ] Challenge yourself with a new project. It doesn't have to be difficult: Do something that you enjoy and allows you to express yourself. Examples are writing, painting, etc.

- [ ] Do something that will make you relax. Listen to soft music, read a good book, take a warm bath or shower, do relaxation exercises.

- [ ] Talk to an understanding friend, relative, clergyman, or co-worker who will allow you to vent the tensions and frustrations that you are experiencing.

⑨ Enlarged Prostate

If they live long enough, most men will eventually get an enlarged prostate gland. Doctors call it benign prostatic hypertrophy. The prostate gland is a walnut-shaped organ located below a man's bladder that makes seminal fluid. It actually surrounds a portion of the bladder and the beginning of the urethra, the tube that carries urine away from the bladder.

An enlarged prostate is usually not cancerous or life threatening. It may cause some problems such as:

☐ Increased urgency to urinate.

☐ Frequent urination, especially during the night.

☐ Delay in onset of urine flow.

☐ Diminished or slow stream of urine flow.

☐ Incomplete emptying of the bladder.

These symptoms indicate that the prostate gland has enlarged enough to partially obstruct the flow of urine. Serious complications, such as kidney damage or kidney infection, could occur. Part of or all of the prostate gland can be removed by surgery if it becomes so enlarged that it interferes with the flow of urine. The surgery is called transurethral resection of the prostate (TURP). A new laser-assisted surgery has been approved by the FDA but requires special training for physicians performing it, so it is not yet done as often as the traditional TURP surgery.

Prostate surgery can result in impotence and/or incontinence. It is important to discuss the benefits and the risks of this operation with your doctor.

An enlarged prostate does not necessarily indicate the presence of prostate cancer. A blood test called PSA, which stands for prostate specific antigen, can be done along with a digital rectal exam to help detect prostate cancer. According to the American Cancer Society, these two tests should be done annually on men over 50 years of age. *[Note: Many other advisory groups and experts though, do not recommend a PSA test for screening men who have not shown symptoms of prostate cancer.]*

Another test called transrectal ultrasound, which uses sound waves to show the structure around the prostate gland can also be done. A combination of all three tests best predicts prostate cancer.

Enlarged Prostate, continued

Questions To Ask

Are you experiencing one or more of the following symptoms? Some of these could indicate an enlarged prostate. Some point to the possibility of an infection of the prostate.
- **Burning, frequent or painful urination.**
- **Inability to urinate.**
- **Pain in the lower back, groin, or testicles.**
- **Pain in or near the penis.**
- **Pain on ejaculation.**
- **Discharge from the penis (blood or pus).**
- **Fever and/or shaking chills.**

YES → SEE DOCTOR

NO

PROVIDE SELF-CARE

Self-Care Procedures

☐ Remain sexually active.

☐ Take hot baths.

☐ Avoid dampness and cold temperatures.

☐ Do not let the bladder get too full. Urinate as soon as the urge arises. Relax when you urinate.

☐ When you take long car trips, make frequent stops to urinate. Keep a container in the car, that you can urinate in when you can't get to a bathroom in time.

☐ Whenever possible, sit on a hard chair instead of a soft one.

☐ Limit coffee, tea, alcohol, and foods that are spicy.

☐ Drink eight or more glasses of water every day.

☐ Reduce stress.

☐ Don't smoke.

☐ Avoid taking over-the-counter antihistamines.

10 Fever

Fever is one way the body fights infection. It helps speed up the body's defense actions by increasing blood flow. A fever in an older person can sometimes cause more problems than in younger persons. A high fever, for example, can put an extra strain on the heart. This could trigger heart failure for an older person with heart disease.

Fevers are also more likely to cause delirium or disorientation in older adults than in younger people. Thus, it is important that older persons take their temperature and note other symptoms if they think they have a fever. What is an elevated temperature? Although 98.6°F has been considered normal for years, a recent study has stated that normal body temperature may range from 97°F to 100°F.

Body temperature even fluctuates throughout the day. It's usually lowest in the morning and highest in the late afternoon and evening. Where you measure your temperature also makes a difference. Rectal readings are usually more accurate and read a degree higher than oral readings.

Taking your temperature by mouth after you drink a hot liquid like soup or tea can mislead you into thinking you have a fever when you don't.

Other factors that can temporarily affect your temperature include:

☐ Wearing too much clothing, if you're over-dressed enough to raise your body temperature.

☐ Exercise.

☐ Hot, humid weather.

Typically, in a older adult, if having a fever up to 102°F causes no harm or discomfort, and you have no other medical problems, it may require no treatment. But if the fever is making you uncomfortable, is 102°F or higher, or if you are frail, or have a medical condition, you should treat it.

Know too, that the body can lose some of its ability to generate a fever as it ages. You could have an infection with no elevation in temperature when you are older, whereas, you probably would have had a fever with the same infection when you were younger. Older adults should, therefore, be mindful of other signs of infection such as headache, swelling, redness, restlessness, confusion, etc., even when the thermometer reads normal. In addition, a temperature reading of 97°F - 98°F or lower could also be a sign of an infection in an older person. Knowing what your normal temperature is and when you go above or below that is a better way to determine illness.

Fever, continued

Questions to Ask

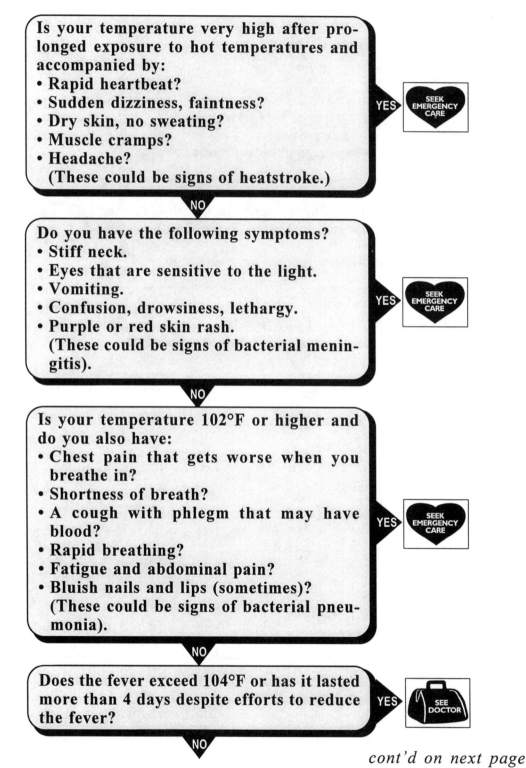

Is your temperature very high after prolonged exposure to hot temperatures and accompanied by:
- Rapid heartbeat?
- Sudden dizziness, faintness?
- Dry skin, no sweating?
- Muscle cramps?
- Headache?
(These could be signs of heatstroke.)

YES → SEEK EMERGENCY CARE

NO

Do you have the following symptoms?
- Stiff neck.
- Eyes that are sensitive to the light.
- Vomiting.
- Confusion, drowsiness, lethargy.
- Purple or red skin rash.
(These could be signs of bacterial meningitis).

YES → SEEK EMERGENCY CARE

NO

Is your temperature 102°F or higher and do you also have:
- Chest pain that gets worse when you breathe in?
- Shortness of breath?
- A cough with phlegm that may have blood?
- Rapid breathing?
- Fatigue and abdominal pain?
- Bluish nails and lips (sometimes)?
(These could be signs of bacterial pneumonia).

YES → SEEK EMERGENCY CARE

NO

Does the fever exceed 104°F or has it lasted more than 4 days despite efforts to reduce the fever?

YES → SEE DOCTOR

NO

cont'd on next page

Fever, continued

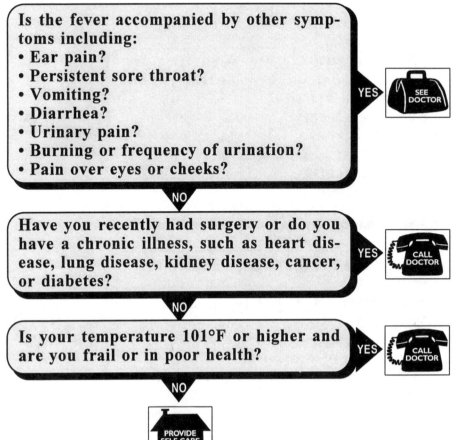

Is the fever accompanied by other symptoms including:
- **Ear pain?**
- **Persistent sore throat?**
- **Vomiting?**
- **Diarrhea?**
- **Urinary pain?**
- **Burning or frequency of urination?**
- **Pain over eyes or cheeks?**

YES → SEE DOCTOR

NO ↓

Have you recently had surgery or do you have a chronic illness, such as heart disease, lung disease, kidney disease, cancer, or diabetes?

YES → CALL DOCTOR

NO ↓

Is your temperature 101°F or higher and are you frail or in poor health?

YES → CALL DOCTOR

NO ↓

PROVIDE SELF-CARE

Self-Care Procedures

Drink at least 1½ to 2 quarts of liquids every day. This includes water, fruit juice, etc. Do check with your doctor first, though, if you have kidney disease or congestive heart failure.

☐ Take a sponge bath with tepid (about 70°F) water. (Sponging with alcohol has no advantage and often makes people feel ill, because of alcohol's pungent odor.)

☐ For high fevers, put cold packs or cool wash cloths on the neck, groin and under the armpits.

☐ Take the right dose of aspirin or acetaminophen for your age every 3 or 4 hours.

☐ Get plenty of bed rest.

☐ Don't bundle up in heavy clothing or several layers of blankets.

☐ Avoid strenuous activity, especially when outdoors.

☐ Avoid being outside in hot, humid weather. Air out hot cars before riding in them. Use air-conditioning in the car and home whenever possible to avoid getting over heated.

⑪ Flu

"Oh, it's just a touch of the flu," some say, as if they had nothing more than a cold. Yet each year, 50,000 people die from pneumonia and other complications of the flu virus. Older adults are especially at risk for flu complications if they are 65 or older, frail, and/or have:

- ☐ A chronic lung disease such as emphysema or bronchitis.

- ☐ Heart disease.

- ☐ Anemia.

- ☐ Diabetes.

- ☐ A weakened immune system from an illness, treatments (Example: Chemotherapy) and/or medications (Example: Steroids).

Cold and flu symptoms resemble each other, but they differ in intensity. A cold generally starts out with some minor sniffling and sneezing, but the flu hits you all at once. You're fine one hour and in bed the next. A cold rarely moves into the lungs. The flu can cause pneumonia. You may be able to carry on your normal routine with a cold, but with the flu you may be too ill to leave your bed.

If the following symptoms come on suddenly and intensely, you probably have the flu:

- ☐ Dry cough.

- ☐ Sore throat, hoarseness, runny nose.

- ☐ Severe headache.

- ☐ General muscle aches or backache.

- ☐ Extreme fatigue, loss of appetite.

- ☐ Chills.

- ☐ Fever up to 104°F.

- ☐ Pain when you move your eyes, or a burning sensation in the eyes.

- ☐ Chest pain.

The most telling symptoms in that list are extreme fatigue and muscle aches. These are normally absent with a cold.

Prevention

To avoid getting the flu in the first place, medical authorities recommend an influenza vaccination before each flu season for people over age 65 or anyone with a chronic medical illness that would hinder their ability to fight off the flu on their own. The influenza vaccine should be given in September, October or November of each year. Also, get plenty of rest, eat well, and exercise to stay strong and fight off the flu.

Flu, continued

Be aware that a separate or recent illness, as well as aging itself, can lower your resistance, making it easier for you to pick up the flu if you are exposed to a flu virus. Therefore, avoid contact with others who have the flu or other upper respiratory infections. Wash your hands often. Keep your hands away from your eyes, nose and mouth.

Medical treatment may be necessary for persons over 50 who have the flu, especially for those mentioned earlier, who are at risk of complications from this influenza virus. Besides the recommended annual vaccine, the anti-viral drugs Amantadine or Ramantadine may be prescribed. *[Note: In order for Ramantadine to be effective, it must be taken within the first 48 hours of the onset of symptoms of the flu.]* Antibiotics (to combat any bacterial infection, if also present) and other prescription medicines aimed at relieving flu symptoms, may also be given by your doctor.

Questions to Ask

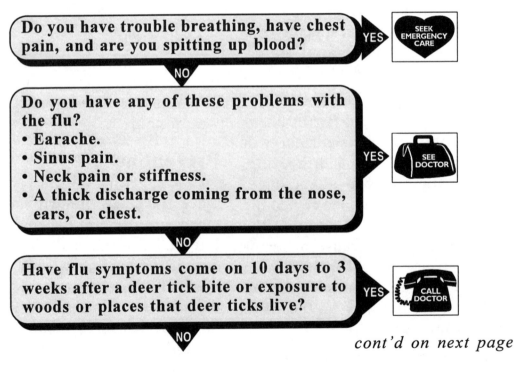

Do you have trouble breathing, have chest pain, and are you spitting up blood? **YES** → SEEK EMERGENCY CARE

NO

Do you have any of these problems with the flu?
- Earache.
- Sinus pain.
- Neck pain or stiffness.
- A thick discharge coming from the nose, ears, or chest.

YES → SEE DOCTOR

NO

Have flu symptoms come on 10 days to 3 weeks after a deer tick bite or exposure to woods or places that deer ticks live? **YES** → CALL DOCTOR

NO

cont'd on next page

Flu, continued

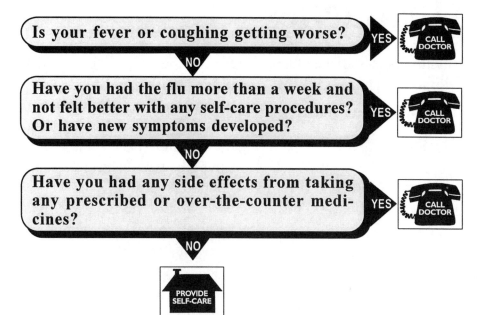

Is your fever or coughing getting worse? **YES** → **CALL DOCTOR**

NO

Have you had the flu more than a week and not felt better with any self-care procedures? Or have new symptoms developed? **YES** → **CALL DOCTOR**

NO

Have you had any side effects from taking any prescribed or over-the-counter medicines? **YES** → **CALL DOCTOR**

NO

PROVIDE SELF-CARE

Self-Care Procedures

There's no cure for the flu. It has to run its course. The goal then, is to minimize discomfort and prevent complications. Generally, if you are in good health, you can treat the flu on your own. The best way to do that is to get plenty of rest, so your body can fight off the virus. Try these tips too:

☐ Drink lots of hot (not scalding) drinks. They soothe your throat, help unplug your nose and put back water you lose by sweating.

☐ Gargle with warm, strong tea or warm, salt water.

☐ Suck on lozenges or hard candies to lubricate your throat.

☐ Let yourself cough if you are bringing up mucus. Don't suppress a cough that produces mucus. Ask your pharmacist for an over-the-counter expectorant if this is all right with your doctor. Also, if mucus is bloody, yellow or green, contact your physician for advice.

☐ Don't drink milk or eat dairy products for a couple of days. They make mucus thick and hard to cough up in some persons.

☐ Wash your hands often, especially after blowing your nose and before handling food. This also helps you avoid spreading the flu virus to others.

☐ Take acetaminophen, aspirin, ibuprofen or naproxen sodium if allowed by your doctor.

⑫ Headaches

There are many causes of headaches in older persons. These include:

☐ Tension, fatigue and stress.

☐ Sensitivity to certain foods and drinks.

☐ Exposure to chemicals from alcohol, cigarette smoke, pollution and poison.

☐ A side effect of some medications. (Example: Nitroglycerin, after taken for angina).

☐ Health conditions that include:

- Allergies.
- Colds, flu or other infections.
- Dental problems.
- Depression.
- Earaches.
- High blood pressure.
- Hunger or low blood sugar.
- Menopause.
- Shingles. (Headaches can be more intense following the acute attack).
- Sinus problems.
- Sore throats.

Headaches caused by tension, fatigue, stress, and food and beverage sensitivities can be dealt with using prevention and self-care procedures. (See page 45 and 48).

Headaches that are symptoms of other health conditions are relieved when the condition is treated successfully. Pain relievers, either over-the-counter (OTC) ones or ones prescribed by your doctor, can reduce headache pain. [Note: Check with your doctor about which OTC pain reliever is best for you. Aspirin, for example, may not be a good choice if you have an ulcer or take a blood thinner medicine.]

Sometimes, a headache can be a symptom of a health problem that is serious such as:

☐ Acute glaucoma.

☐ Stroke.

☐ Transient ischemic attack (TIA), a temporary "mini-stroke".

☐ Aneurysm.

☐ Giant cell (temporal) arteritis (chronic inflammation of certain blood vessels, often in the temple region).

☐ Brain tumor.

Fortunately, less than 10% of headaches are caused by serious conditions. Prompt medical care is needed for these. (See Questions to Ask).

Tension or muscular headaches are very common. Unconscious tensing of the face, neck, or scalp muscles produces a dull, relentless ache. You

Headaches, continued

feel the pressure in your forehead, temples, or around the back of the head, where the muscles of your upper back attach. Lack of sleep or the stress of everyday hassles can trigger tension headaches. Doing tedious work or reading frequently can cause muscular headaches.

Even though migraine headaches are more common in younger persons, especially in women between the ages of 30 and 49, persons over 50 do experience them. Migraines tend to run in families, and are more debilitating than tension headaches. They usually start on one side of the head and throb. They are caused in part by changes (narrowing and widening) of blood vessels in the brain. Vomiting, nausea, blurred vision, flashing spots, sensitivity to light, and ringing in the ears often accompany migraines.

Sinus headaches are noted by pain over the sinuses of the face, in the area of your upper cheekbones, forehead, and the bridge of your nose. Inflammation and fluid buildup cause the pain, and bending over or touching the affected area seems to aggravate it. Colds, allergies, air pollution, and other respiratory problems can trigger a sinus headache.

Prevention

To prevent headaches from recurring:

☐ Try to anticipate when pain will strike. Keep a headache journal that records when, where, and why headaches seem to occur.

☐ Note early symptoms and try to abort a headache in its earliest stages. Take pain medicine such as acetaminophen right away.

☐ Exercise regularly. This seems to keep headaches at bay.

☐ Avoid foods and beverages known to trigger headaches in sensitive people. Try to figure out which foods and beverages affect you.

Particularly troublesome foods may include:

☐ Alcoholic beverages, especially red wine.

☐ Aspartame (the artificial sweetener in NutraSweet™).

☐ Bananas.

☐ Caffeine from coffee, tea, cola soft drinks, or some medications.

☐ Chicken livers.

☐ Chocolate.

☐ Citrus fruits such as grapefruit, lemon, limes, oranges.

☐ Cured meats such as frankfurters.

Headaches, continued

- ☐ Food additives such as mono-sodium glutamate or MSG.
- ☐ Hard cheeses such as aged cheddar or provolone.
- ☐ Herring.
- ☐ Lima Beans.
- ☐ Nuts.
- ☐ Onions.
- ☐ Sour cream.
- ☐ Vinegar.

Questions to Ask

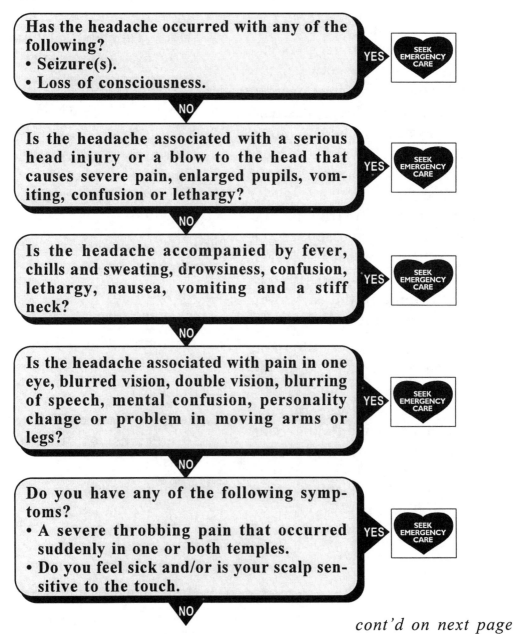

Has the headache occurred with any of the following?
- **Seizure(s).**
- **Loss of consciousness.**

YES → SEEK EMERGENCY CARE

NO

Is the headache associated with a serious head injury or a blow to the head that causes severe pain, enlarged pupils, vomiting, confusion or lethargy?

YES → SEEK EMERGENCY CARE

NO

Is the headache accompanied by fever, chills and sweating, drowsiness, confusion, lethargy, nausea, vomiting and a stiff neck?

YES → SEEK EMERGENCY CARE

NO

Is the headache associated with pain in one eye, blurred vision, double vision, blurring of speech, mental confusion, personality change or problem in moving arms or legs?

YES → SEEK EMERGENCY CARE

NO

Do you have any of the following symptoms?
- **A severe throbbing pain that occurred suddenly in one or both temples.**
- **Do you feel sick and/or is your scalp sensitive to the touch.**

YES → SEEK EMERGENCY CARE

NO

cont'd on next page

Headaches, continued

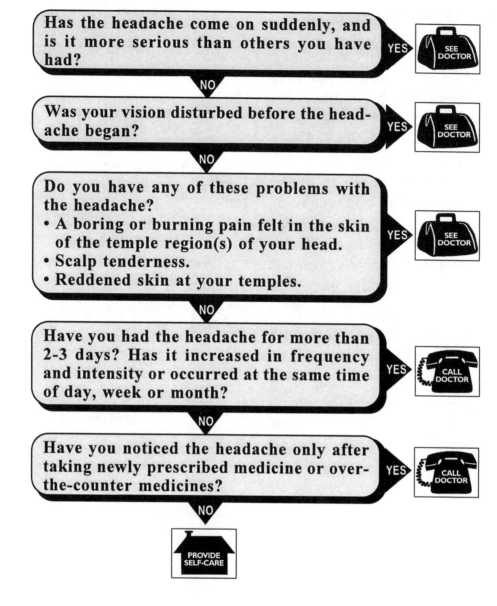

Has the headache come on suddenly, and is it more serious than others you have had?

YES → SEE DOCTOR

NO

Was your vision disturbed before the headache began?

YES → SEE DOCTOR

NO

Do you have any of these problems with the headache?
- A boring or burning pain felt in the skin of the temple region(s) of your head.
- Scalp tenderness.
- Reddened skin at your temples.

YES → SEE DOCTOR

NO

Have you had the headache for more than 2-3 days? Has it increased in frequency and intensity or occurred at the same time of day, week or month?

YES → CALL DOCTOR

NO

Have you noticed the headache only after taking newly prescribed medicine or over-the-counter medicines?

YES → CALL DOCTOR

NO

PROVIDE SELF-CARE

Headaches, continued
Self-Care Procedures

For on-the-spot headache relief:

☐ Take the over-the-counter pain reliever such as acetaminophen, aspirin, ibuprofen or naproxen sodium that your doctor suggests you use, and according to his or her directions. Do so at the beginning of the headache. Or take medicine prescribed by your doctor. Remind your doctor of any other medicines you are taking. This includes over-the-counter and prescription ones.

☐ Rest in a quiet, dark room with your eyes closed.

☐ Massage the base of your skull with your thumbs. Work from the ears toward the center of the back of your head.

☐ Also, massage both temples, your shoulders, neck and jaw gently.

☐ Take a warm bath or shower.

☐ Place a cold or warm washcloth, whichever feels better, over the area that aches.

☐ Practice a relaxation technique such as visualizing a serene setting, meditating, or deep breathing.

13 Hearing Loss

Do people seem to mumble a lot lately? Do you have trouble hearing in church, in theaters, at the dinner table or at family gatherings? Does your family keep asking you to turn down the volume on the TV or radio?

These are signs of gradual, age-related hearing loss called presbycusis. High pitched sounds are the ones to go first. Hearing loss from presbycusis cannot be corrected, but hearing aids, along with the self-care procedures listed on page 51 can be helpful.

Hearing loss can also result from other things:

☐ Acoustic trauma - this may be caused by a blow to the ear or from excessive noise, especially if exposed to it for long periods of time. Examples of excessive noise sources are chain saws, power mowers, gunfire and loud machinery.

☐ Blood vessel disorders including high blood pressure.

☐ A blood clot that travels to the acoustic nerves in the ear.

☐ Ear wax that blocks the ear canal.

☐ Chronic middle ear infections, or an infection of the inner ear.

☐ Meniere's disease (a disease marked by excess fluid in canals of the inner ear which helps maintain balance).

☐ Oteosclerosis - (a hereditary bone problem in the middle ear).

☐ Multiple sclerosis.

☐ Syphilis.

☐ Brain tumor.

Hair cell damage in the ear can be experienced between the ages of 20 and 40 and continues with aging. These hair cells cannot be replaced or restored once damaged. The result can be hearing loss. Coordination and balance can also become impaired.

If you have hearing loss, consult your doctor. He or she may test for and diagnose the problem or send you to a specialist, such as an ear-nose-and throat doctor or a certified audiologist. A certified audiologist tests and treats persons who have hearing and related problems.

Hearing Loss, continued

Questions to Ask

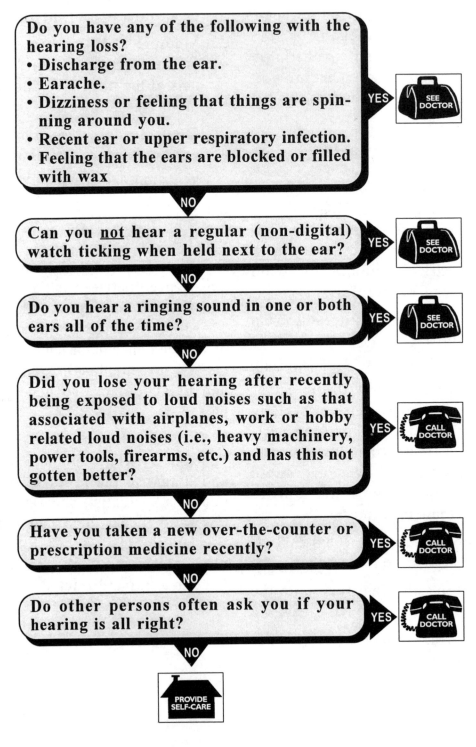

Do you have any of the following with the hearing loss?
- Discharge from the ear.
- Earache.
- Dizziness or feeling that things are spinning around you.
- Recent ear or upper respiratory infection.
- Feeling that the ears are blocked or filled with wax

YES → SEE DOCTOR

NO

Can you **not** hear a regular (non-digital) watch ticking when held next to the ear?

YES → SEE DOCTOR

NO

Do you hear a ringing sound in one or both ears all of the time?

YES → SEE DOCTOR

NO

Did you lose your hearing after recently being exposed to loud noises such as that associated with airplanes, work or hobby related loud noises (i.e., heavy machinery, power tools, firearms, etc.) and has this not gotten better?

YES → CALL DOCTOR

NO

Have you taken a new over-the-counter or prescription medicine recently?

YES → CALL DOCTOR

NO

Do other persons often ask you if your hearing is all right?

YES → CALL DOCTOR

NO

PROVIDE SELF-CARE

Hearing Loss, continued
Self-Care Procedures

For gradual, age-related hearing loss (presbycusis):

☐ Ask people to speak clearly, distinctly, and in a normal tone.

☐ Look at people when they are talking to you. Watch their expressions to help you understand what they are saying. Ask them to face you.

☐ Try to limit background noise when having a conversation.

☐ In a church or theater, sit near the front, but not in the front row. Rather, sit in the third or forth row with people surrounding you.

☐ Install a buzzer, flasher, or amplifier on your telephone, door chime, and alarm clock. Also, an audiologist may be able to show you other techniques for "training" yourself to hear better.

☐ If a hearing aid is prescribed, learn to use and wear it properly.

☐ See a certified audiologist for a diagnostic hearing evaluation. An audiologist can decide if a hearing aid can help you.

To Clear Ear Wax:

☐ Use an over-the-counter cleaner such as Murine Ear Drops, Debrox, or the name brand, Audiologist's Choice. Follow package directions.

☐ Or, lie on your side or tilt your head sideways. Using a clean syringe or medicine dropper, carefully squeeze a few drops of lukewarm water into your ear (or have someone else do this). Let the water remain there for 10-15 minutes and then tilt the head to allow it to drain out of the ear. After several minutes, follow the same procedure using warm water again. You can repeat this entire procedure again in three hours if the ear is not yet clear.

☐ Don't try to remove ear wax by poking a pointed object into your ear to scrape it out. You could put a hole in your eardrum or damage the skin of your ear canal.

To prevent hearing loss or hearing impairment:

☐ Get proper medical treatment for disorders that can cause hearing loss (Example: High blood pressure, Meniere's disease, etc.).

☐ Don't put cotton-tipped swabs, fingers, bobby pins, etc. in your ear.

☐ Do not blow your nose with too much force. It is better to "gently" blow one nostril at a time

Hearing Loss, continued

with a tissue or handkerchief held loosely over the nostrils.

☐ Avoid places that have loud noises (airports, construction sites, etc.). Protect your ears with earplugs.

☐ Avoid excessive use or overdosing on drugs that can cause hearing impairment. (Example: Heavy use of aspirin or quinine).

Also be aware of things that can help you to hear sounds if your hearing is impaired.

☐ Hearing aids (See your doctor and/or a certified audiologist).

☐ Listening devices made to assist you in hearing sounds from the TV and radio.

☐ Special audio equipment that can be installed in your telephone by the telephone company.

☐ Portable devices made especially to amplify sounds. These can be used for movies, classes, meetings, etc.

⑭ Heartburn

The term heartburn is a misnomer. It has nothing to do with the heart. Rather, it involves the esophagus (the tube that connects the throat to the stomach,) and the stomach itself. The esophagus passes behind the breastbone alongside the heart, so the inflammation or irritation that takes place there feels like a burning sensation in the heart.

What causes this irritation? Gastric acids from the stomach splash back up into the lower portion of the esophagus, causing pain. The digestive acids don't harm the stomach, thanks to its protective coating, but the esophagus has no such armor which results in discomfort.

Heartburn may be more frequent in persons over 50 because the muscles of the esophagus decrease in strength with aging. Also, older persons often don't drink enough water, which could add to the problem.

The most common heartburn triggers are:

☐ Taking aspirin, ibuprofen, naproxen sodium, arthritis medicine, or cortisone.

☐ Eating heavy meals or eating rapidly.

☐ Eating foods like chocolate, garlic, onions, peppermint, tomatoes or citrus fruits.

☐ Smoking.

☐ Drinking coffee (regular or decaffeinated).

☐ Drinking alcohol.

☐ Obesity.

☐ Swallowing too much air.

☐ Stress.

☐ A weakened or malfunctioning valve between the esophagus and the stomach.

☐ A bulging of the upper part of the stomach through the diaphragm. This is called gastroesophageal reflux disease (GERD). It was commonly termed hiatal hernia.

Heartburn, continued

Questions to Ask

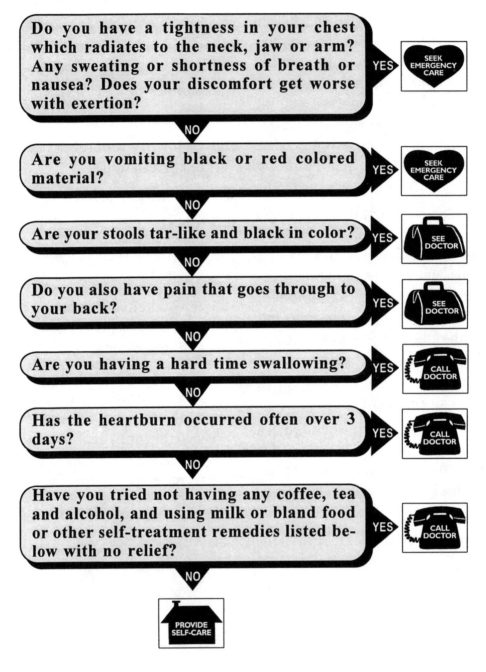

Do you have a tightness in your chest which radiates to the neck, jaw or arm? Any sweating or shortness of breath or nausea? Does your discomfort get worse with exertion? **YES** → SEEK EMERGENCY CARE

NO

Are you vomiting black or red colored material? **YES** → SEEK EMERGENCY CARE

NO

Are your stools tar-like and black in color? **YES** → SEE DOCTOR

NO

Do you also have pain that goes through to your back? **YES** → SEE DOCTOR

NO

Are you having a hard time swallowing? **YES** → CALL DOCTOR

NO

Has the heartburn occurred often over 3 days? **YES** → CALL DOCTOR

NO

Have you tried not having any coffee, tea and alcohol, and using milk or bland food or other self-treatment remedies listed below with no relief? **YES** → CALL DOCTOR

NO

PROVIDE SELF-CARE

Heartburn, continued

Self-Care Procedures

Treatment consists of avoiding as many contributing factors as possible, plus the following:

☐ Sit straight, and stand up or walk around whenever you can. Bending over or lying down after eating makes it too easy for gastric secretions to move up to the esophagus.

☐ If heartburn bothers you at night, raise the head of the bed slightly. (Example: Put the head of your bed up on 6 inch blocks, or buy a wedge especially made for putting between the mattress and box spring).

☐ Lose weight if you are overweight.

☐ Avoid wearing tight-fitting garments around the abdomen. (Example: girdle).

☐ Eat small meals.

☐ Limit foods and drinks that contain air. (Example: Baked goods, waffles, whipped cream, carbonated beverages).

☐ Don't drink through straws or bottles with narrow mouths.

☐ Don't eat for 2 to 3 hours before bedtime.

☐ If other treatments fail, take an antacid. They coat your stomach and neutralize acids. Take 1 to 2 tablespoons of a non-absorbable liquid antacid such as magnesium hydroxide every 2 to 4 hours. Don't take antacids on a regular basis, unless you first check with your doctor. *[Note: People with heart disease, kidney disease, or high blood pressure or anyone taking any prescription medicine should consult a physician before taking antacids.]*

☐ Don't take sodium bicarbonate (baking soda). It may neutralize stomach acid at first, but when its effects wear off, the acid comes back to a greater degree causing severe gastric acid rebound.

☐ Don't smoke. It promotes heartburn.

☐ If you do take aspirin, ibuprofen, naproxen sodium or arthritis medicines, take them with food.

⑮ Insomnia

Do you ever find yourself wide awake long after you go to bed at night? Well, you're not alone. About 40 million Americans are bothered by insomnia. They either have trouble falling asleep at night, wake up in the middle of the night, or wake up too early and can't get back to sleep. And when they're not asleep, insomniacs worry about whether or not they'll be able to sleep. They are also often irritable and have fatigue during the day.

Having a sleepless night once in awhile is nothing to lose sleep over. But if insomnia bothers you for three weeks or longer, it may be a real medical problem. Some medical problems that lead to insomnia include:

☐ Over-activity of the thyroid gland.

☐ Heart or lung conditions that cause shortness of breath when lying down.

☐ Depression, anxiety disorders.

☐ Allergies and early-morning wheezing.

☐ Any condition, illness, injury or surgery that causes pain and/or discomfort, such as arthritis, which interrupts sleep.

☐ Restless leg syndrome (RLS), a condition which results in in-voluntary jerking movement of the legs.

☐ Sexual problems (Example: Impotence).

☐ Hot flashes that interrupt sleep.

☐ Any disorder (urinary, gastrointestinal or neurological) that makes it necessary to urinate or have a bowel movement during the night.

☐ Side effects of certain medications. (Examples: Decongestants, cortisone drugs).

Other things that lead to insomnia:

☐ Emotional stress.

☐ Too much noise when falling asleep. This includes a snoring partner.

☐ The use of stimulants such as caffeine from coffee, tea or colas and stay awake pills such as NoDoz.

☐ A lack of physical exercise.

☐ Lack of a sex partner.

Once the problem that leads to the insomnia is found and treated, the insomnia usually goes away.

You should check with your doctor before taking sleeping pills. They can help in some cases as a temporary form of relief. They can, though, with regular use, lead to

Insomnia, continued

rebound insomnia. This happens when you quit taking sleeping pills and the insomnia returns. If your doctor does prescribe sleep medicine, make sure you take it as directed. Let your doctor know if you have any side effects like dizziness, hallucinations, confusion, etc. Also, don't take anyone else's sleeping pills.

Questions To Ask

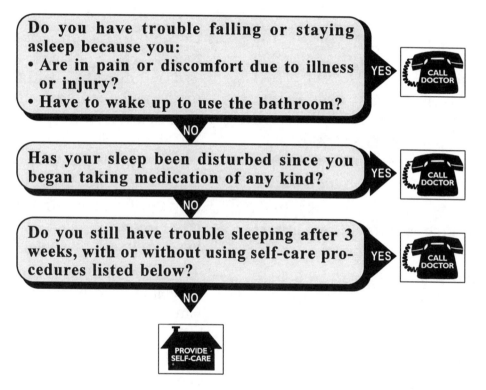

Do you have trouble falling or staying asleep because you:
- **Are in pain or discomfort due to illness or injury?**
- **Have to wake up to use the bathroom?**

YES — CALL DOCTOR

NO

Has your sleep been disturbed since you began taking medication of any kind?

YES — CALL DOCTOR

NO

Do you still have trouble sleeping after 3 weeks, with or without using self-care procedures listed below?

YES — CALL DOCTOR

NO

PROVIDE SELF-CARE

Self-Care Procedures

Many old-fashioned remedies for sleeplessness work, and work well. Next time you find yourself unable to sleep, try these time-tested cures.

☐ Avoid caffeine in all forms after lunchtime. Coffee, tea,, chocolate, colas, and some other soft drinks contain this stimulant, as do certain over-the-counter and prescription medicines. Check over-the-counter medicine labels for caffeine content.

☐ Avoid long naps during the day. Naps decrease the quality of nighttime sleep.

Insomnia, continued

- [ ] Avoid more than one or two servings of alcoholic beverages at dinner time and during the rest of the evening. Even though alcohol is a sedative, it can disrupt sleep. Always check with your doctor about using alcohol, if you are taking medications.

- [ ] Have food items rich in the amino acid L-tryptophan such as milk, turkey or tuna fish before you go to bed. Eating foods with carbohydrates such as cereal, breads and fruits may help as well. Do not, however, take L-tryptophan supplements.

- [ ] Get regular exercise but don't exercise within a few hours before going to bed.

- [ ] Take a nice, long, warm bath before bedtime. This soothes and unwinds tense muscles, leaving you relaxed enough to fall asleep.

- [ ] Read a book or do some type of repetitive, calm activity. Avoid distractions that may hold your attention and keep you awake such as watching a suspense movie when you are trying to fall asleep.

- [ ] Make your bedroom as comfortable as possible. Create a quiet, dark atmosphere. Use clean, fresh sheets and pillows, and keep the room temperature comfortable (neither too warm nor too cool.)

- [ ] Ban worry from the bedroom. Don't allow yourself to rehash the mistakes of the day as you toss and turn. You're off duty now. The idea is to associate your bed with sleep.

- [ ] Develop a regular bedtime routine. Locking or checking doors and windows, brushing your teeth, and reading before you turn in every night primes you for sleep.

- [ ] Count those sheep! Counting slowly is a soothing, hypnotic activity. By picturing repetitive, monotonous images, you may bore yourself to sleep.

- [ ] Try listening to recordings made especially to help promote sleep. Check local bookstores.

- [ ] Try taking Melatonin, a product you can get from a health food store. It appears to help some people sleep better and is relatively safe. Take as directed on the label.

- [ ] If you've tried to fall asleep, but are still awake after 30 minutes, get up and sit quietly in another room for about 20 minutes. Then, go back to bed. Repeat this as many times as you need to, until you are able to fall asleep.

⑯ Menopause

Menopause is when a woman's menstrual periods stop. It signals the end of fertility. A woman is said to have gone through menopause when her menstrual periods have stopped for an entire year. "The change", as menopause is often called, generally occurs between the ages of 45 and 55. It can, though, take place as early as 35 or as late as 65. It can also result from the surgical removal of both ovaries.

The physical and emotional signs and symptoms that go with menopause usually span 1 - 2 years or more (peri-menopause). They vary from woman to woman. The changes themselves are a result of a number of factors. These include hormone changes such as estrogen decline, the aging process itself, and stress.

Physical signs and symptoms associated with menopause are:

☐ Hot flashes - sudden waves of heat that can start at the waist or chest and work their way to the neck and face and sometimes the rest of the body. They are more common in the evening and during hot weather. They can hit as often as every 90 minutes. Each one can last from 15 seconds to 30 minutes - five minutes is average. Seventy-five to eighty percent of women going through menopause experience hot flashes, some more bothered by them than others. Sometimes heart palpitations accompany hot flashes.

☐ Menstrual changes - this varies and can include:

• Periods that get shorter and lighter for two or more years.

• Periods that stop for a few months and then start up again and are more widely spaced.

• Periods that bring heavy bleeding and/or the passage of many or large blood clots. This can lead to anemia.

☐ Vaginal dryness - this results from hormone changes. The vaginal wall also becomes thinner. These can make sexual intercourse painful or uncomfortable and can lead to irritation and increased risk for infection.

☐ Loss of bladder tone which can result in stress incontinence - leaking urine when you cough, sneeze, laugh, exercise or lift heavy objects. (See Urinary Incontinence on page 80).

59

Menopause, continued

- ☐ Headaches, dizziness.
- ☐ Skin and hair changes. Skin is more likely to wrinkle. Growth of facial hair, but thinning of hair in the temple region.
- ☐ Breast tenderness.
- ☐ Bloating in upper abdomen.
- ☐ Muscles lose some strength and tone.
- ☐ Bones become more brittle increasing the risk for osteoporosis.
- ☐ Risk for a heart attack increases when estrogen levels drop.

Emotional changes associated with menopause:

- ☐ Irritability.
- ☐ Mood changes.
- ☐ Lack of concentration, difficulty with memory.
- ☐ Tension, anxiety, depression.
- ☐ Insomnia which may result from hot flashes that interrupt sleep.

Treatment for menopause varies from woman to woman. If symptoms cause little or no distress, medical treatment may not be needed. Self-care procedures (see page 62) may be all that is required. Hormone replacement therapy (HRT) can reduce many of the symptoms of menopause. It also offers significant protection against osteoporosis and heart disease. Each woman should discuss the benefits and risks of HRT with her doctor. Medication to treat depression and/or anxiety may be warranted in some women. Also, certain sedative medicines can help with hot flashes.

Questions to Ask

During peri-menopause, do you have any of these?
- **Extreme pain during intercourse.**
- **Pain or burning when urinating.**
- **Thick, white or colored vaginal discharge.**
- **Fever, chills.**

YES ▶ CALL DOCTOR

NO

cont'd on next page

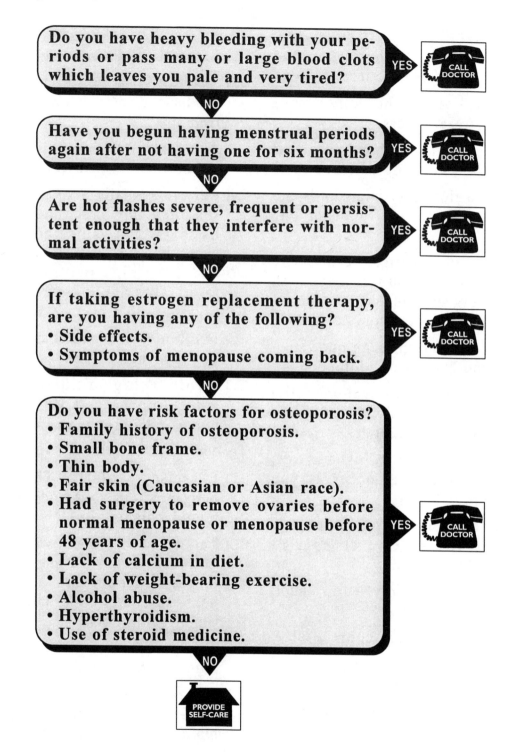

Do you have heavy bleeding with your periods or pass many or large blood clots which leaves you pale and very tired? **YES** → CALL DOCTOR

NO

Have you begun having menstrual periods again after not having one for six months? **YES** → CALL DOCTOR

NO

Are hot flashes severe, frequent or persistent enough that they interfere with normal activities? **YES** → CALL DOCTOR

NO

If taking estrogen replacement therapy, are you having any of the following?
• Side effects.
• Symptoms of menopause coming back. **YES** → CALL DOCTOR

NO

Do you have risk factors for osteoporosis?
• Family history of osteoporosis.
• Small bone frame.
• Thin body.
• Fair skin (Caucasian or Asian race).
• Had surgery to remove ovaries before normal menopause or menopause before 48 years of age.
• Lack of calcium in diet.
• Lack of weight-bearing exercise.
• Alcohol abuse.
• Hyperthyroidism.
• Use of steroid medicine. **YES** → CALL DOCTOR

NO

PROVIDE SELF-CARE

Menopause, continued

Self-Care Procedures

To reduce the discomfort of hot flashes, try these tactics:

- ☐ Wear lightweight clothes made of natural fibers.

- ☐ Limit or avoid beverages that contain caffeine or alcohol.

- ☐ Avoid rich food, spicy foods and large amounts of food at one time.

- ☐ Have cool drinks, especially water, when you feel a hot flash coming on and before and after exercising. Avoid hot drinks.

- ☐ Use relaxation techniques such as meditation or biofeedback.

- ☐ Take 400 international units (IU) of vitamin E daily. Consult your doctor first, though.

- ☐ If you suffer from night sweats, hot flashes that occur as you sleep:
  - • Wear loose fitting cotton nightwear, Have changes of nightwear ready.
  - • Sleep with only a top sheet, not blankets.
  - • Keep the room cool.

To deal with vaginal dryness and painful intercourse:

- ☐ Don't use deodorant soaps or scented products in the vaginal area.

- ☐ Use a water soluble lubricant such as K-Y Jelly to facilitate penetration during intercourse.

- ☐ Avoid oils or petroleum-based products. They encourage infection.

- ☐ Ask your doctor about intra-vaginal estrogen cream.

- ☐ Remain sexually active. Having sex often may lessen the chance of having the vagina constrict, helps keep natural lubrication and maintains pelvic muscle tone. This includes reaching orgasm with a partner or alone.

- ☐ Drink plenty of water daily for healthy vaginal tissues.

- ☐ Avoid using antihistamines unless truly necessary. They dry mucus membranes in the body.

To deal with emotional symptoms:

- ☐ Exercise regularly. This will help maintain your body's hormonal balance.

- ☐ Talk to other women who have gone through or are going through menopause. You can help each other cope with emotional symptoms.

- ☐ Avoid stressful situations as much as possible.

- ☐ Use relaxation techniques. (Examples: Meditation, yoga, listening to soft music, massages).

- ☐ Eat healthy. Check with your doctor about taking vitamin/mineral supplements.

⓱ Shingles

Some things people remember most from their childhood are infectious illnesses such as measles, mumps or chicken pox. One of these infections, chicken pox, may reappear in a different form during adulthood and cause havoc for a second time. Shingles (herpes zoster) is a skin disorder triggered by the chicken pox virus (Varicella zoster) that you first encountered as a child.

This virus is thought to lie dormant in the spinal cord until later in life. Shingles most often occur between the ages of 50 and 70 in both men and women. Even though shingles is not as contagious as chicken pox, infants and people whose immunity is low, should not be exposed to it.

Besides aging, the risks for getting shingles increases with:

❑ Hodgkin's disease or other cancer.

❑ Any illness in which infection-fighting systems are below par.

❑ The use of anti-cancer drugs or any drugs that suppress the immune system (Example: Corticosteroids).

❑ Stress or trauma, either emotional or physical.

Symptoms of shingles include:

❑ Pain, itching, or tingling sensation before the rash appears.

❑ A rash of painful red blisters, which later crust over. Most often, the rash appears on the torso or side of the face but only one side is affected. Shingles is almost never present on both sides of the body. It is serious if it affects the eye because it can lead to blindness.

❑ Though rare, fever and general weakness sometimes occur.

After the crusts fall off (usually within three weeks), pain can persist in the area of the rash. This usually goes away on its own after one to six months. Chronic pain can, however, last for months or years. The older you are, the greater the chances are that this is the case and the recovery time may also take longer.

Most cases of shingles are mild but can result in chronic severe pain, blindness or deafness. So, to be on the safe side, if you get shingles it is wise to let your doctor know.

Shingles, continued

Treatment for shingles includes:

- Pain relief with analgesics. Codeine may sometimes be prescribed.

- Prescription drugs, Famvir, and acyclovir (Zovirax), oral and/or topical ointment, can be very effective. The sooner these medicines are used, the better the results.

- An antibiotic if the blisters become infected.

- Antihistamines.

- Corticosteroids.

- Tranquilizers for a short time.

Questions to Ask

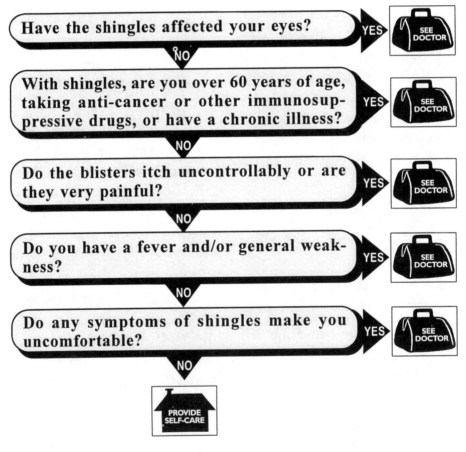

Have the shingles affected your eyes? **YES** → SEE DOCTOR

NO

With shingles, are you over 60 years of age, taking anti-cancer or other immunosuppressive drugs, or have a chronic illness? **YES** → SEE DOCTOR

NO

Do the blisters itch uncontrollably or are they very painful? **YES** → SEE DOCTOR

NO

Do you have a fever and/or general weakness? **YES** → SEE DOCTOR

NO

Do any symptoms of shingles make you uncomfortable? **YES** → SEE DOCTOR

NO

PROVIDE SELF-CARE

Shingles, continued

Self-Care Procedures

Following are things you can do (along with your doctor's treatment plan) to help relieve an active outbreak of shingles:

☐ Take an over-the-counter pain reliever such as acetaminophen, aspirin, ibuprofen or naproxen sodium, unless your doctor has given you prescription pain medicine. *[Note: Ask your doctor which over-the-counter pain medicine is best for you.]*

☐ If possible, keep sores open to the air. Don't bandage them unless you live with or are around children or adults who have not yet had the chicken pox. They could pick up chicken pox from exposure to shingles.

☐ Don't wear restrictive clothing that irritates the area of the body where sores are present.

☐ Wash blisters, but never scrub them.

☐ Apply calamine lotion or baking soda to help alleviate the symptoms.

☐ Avoid drafty areas where you can get chilled.

☐ Put cool compresses on the blisters. You can use several things: A cold cloth or towel dipped in ice water, a bag of frozen vegetables or an ice pack wrapped in a thin towel. Put the cool compress on the blisters for 20 minutes at a time.

18 Shoulder & Neck Pain

Shoulder and neck pain is a common condition in people over age 50. Swinging a golf club, cleaning windows or reaching for a jar, can strain and injure shoulder muscles and tendons, especially in people who are out of condition. Fortunately, this discomfort rarely suggests a serious problem.

Causes of shoulder and neck pain in older people include:

Poor posture and/or awkward sleeping positions - sleeping on a soft mattress can give you a stiff neck the next morning.

Tendinitis - inflammation of a tendon, the cord-like tissue that connects muscles to bone. Left untreated, tendinitis can turn into "frozen shoulder", a stiff, painful condition that may limit your ability to use your shoulder.

Bursitis - an inflammation of the sac (bursa) that encases the shoulder joint. Bursitis can be caused by injury, infection, overuse, arthritis or gout.

Osteoarthritis - unlike rheumatoid arthritis, osteoarthritis develops from normal wear-and-tear of the joints as we age or from repeated injuries. These cause the joints to wear out, producing bony spurs that can press on nerves and cause pain.

Accidents and falls - collarbones can break after falls or auto accidents.

Motor vehicle accidents - you can develop a whiplash injury when your vehicle is hit from behind.

Pinched nerve - arthritis or an injury to your neck can pinch a nerve in your neck. Pain from a pinched nerve usually runs down the arm and one side only.

Tension and stress - when you feel tense, the muscles around your neck can go into spasms.

Sometimes shoulder and neck pain signal serious medical problems, especially with other symptoms such as stiff neck, sudden and severe headache, dizziness, chest pain or pressure, and/or loss of consciousness.

Shoulder & Neck Pain, continued

Prevention

☐ Stretching and strengthening routines, especially before exercising, helps prevent tendinitis. So can using the right equipment and following the proper technique.

☐ Avoid injuries to the shoulder by wearing seat belts in cars and trucks and using protective gear during sporting events.

☐ Avoid vigorous exercise unless you are fit. If you are out of condition, start to strengthen your muscles gradually and slowly increase exercise intensity.

☐ Don't sleep on your stomach. You are likely to twist your neck in this position.

☐ Sleep on a firm polyester pillow or use a special neck (cervical) pillow.

Keep the muscles in your shoulders strong and flexible to prevent injury. These exercises can help:

☐ Stretch the back of your shoulder by reaching with one arm under your chin and across the opposite shoulder, gently push the arm back with the other hand. Hold for 15 seconds. Repeat five times, then switch sides.

☐ Raise one arm and bend it behind your head to touch the opposite shoulder. Use the other hand to gently pull the elbow downward. Hold for 15 seconds. Repeat five times, then switch sides.

☐ Holding light weights, lift your arms out horizontally and slightly forward. Keeping your thumbs toward the floor, slowly lower your arms halfway, then return to shoulder level. Repeat ten times.

☐ Sit straight in a chair. Flex your neck slowly forward and try to touch your chin to your chest. Hold for 10 seconds and go back to the starting position. Repeat five times.

☐ Sit straight in a chair. Look straight ahead. Slowly tilt your head to the right, trying to touch your right ear to your right shoulder. Do not raise your shoulder to meet your ear. Hold for 10 seconds and straighten your head. Repeat five times on this side and then on your left side.

☐ Use a "Water Pic" shower head to massage the neck muscles.

Shoulder & Neck Pain, continued

Questions to Ask

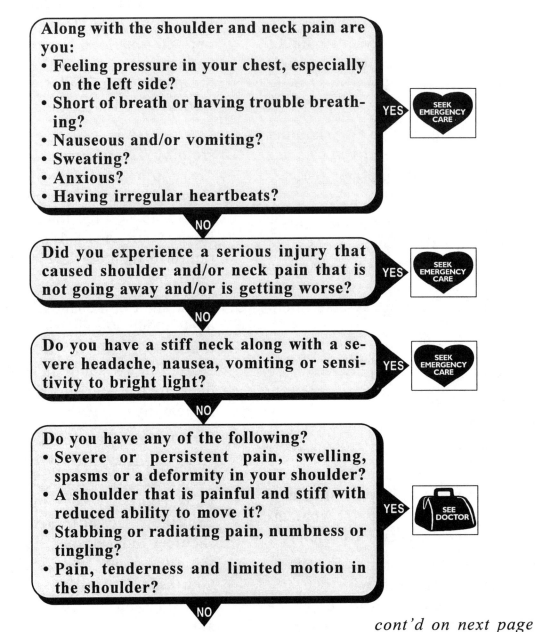

Along with the shoulder and neck pain are you:
- Feeling pressure in your chest, especially on the left side?
- Short of breath or having trouble breathing?
- Nauseous and/or vomiting?
- Sweating?
- Anxious?
- Having irregular heartbeats?

YES → SEEK EMERGENCY CARE

NO ↓

Did you experience a serious injury that caused shoulder and/or neck pain that is not going away and/or is getting worse?

YES → SEEK EMERGENCY CARE

NO ↓

Do you have a stiff neck along with a severe headache, nausea, vomiting or sensitivity to bright light?

YES → SEEK EMERGENCY CARE

NO ↓

Do you have any of the following?
- Severe or persistent pain, swelling, spasms or a deformity in your shoulder?
- A shoulder that is painful and stiff with reduced ability to move it?
- Stabbing or radiating pain, numbness or tingling?
- Pain, tenderness and limited motion in the shoulder?

YES → SEE DOCTOR

NO ↓

cont'd on next page

Shoulder & Neck Pain, continued

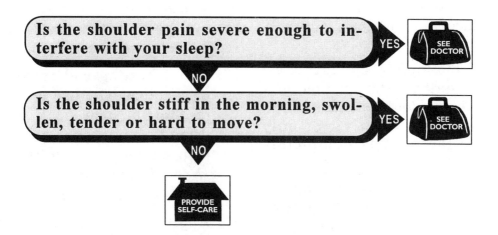

Is the shoulder pain severe enough to interfere with your sleep? YES ▸ SEE DOCTOR

NO

Is the shoulder stiff in the morning, swollen, tender or hard to move? YES ▸ SEE DOCTOR

NO

PROVIDE SELF-CARE

Self-Care Procedures

Unfortunately, no matter how careful people are, injuries do occur. Injured tendons, muscles and ligaments in any part of the body can take a long time to heal. Longer, if fact, than a broken bone. Don't ignore the aches and pains. Studies show that exercising before an injury has healed, may not only worsen it, but may greatly increase the chance for re-injury.

Treating Tendinitis

Taking over-the-counter pain relievers such as aspirin, ibuprofen (i.e., Advil or Motrin) or naproxen sodium (i.e., Aleve) eases the pain and reduces inflammation. Take four to six times a day or as directed by your doctor, if you can tolerate this medication and it doesn't cause problems such as stomach ulcers. Acetaminophen (Tylenol) eases muscle soreness but does not help with inflammation.

[Note: Ask your doctor which pain reliever is right for you.]

Shoulder & Neck Pain, continued

R.I.C.E. is the accepted treatment for tendinitis. While the pain could linger for weeks, with the proper and immediate treatment, it usually disappears in a few days.

R Rest the injured shoulder. Rest stops further inflammation, giving the tendon a chance to heal. Resume your activities only after the pain is completely gone.

I Ice the injured area as soon as possible. Immediately putting ice on the injury helps to speed recovery because it not only relieves pain, but also slows blood flow, reducing internal bleeding and swelling.

- Put ice cubes or crushed ice in a heavy plastic bag with a little water. You can also use a bag of frozen vegetables. Wrap the ice pack in a towel before placing it on the injured areas.

- Apply the ice pack to the injured shoulder for 10 to 20 minutes. Reapply it every two hours and for the next 48 hours during the times you are not sleeping.

C Compress the shoulder injury. Wear a sling to keep the shoulder from moving and to prevent further damage and remind yourself to take it easy.

E Elevate the shoulder whenever possible to further reduce the swelling.

The swelling is usually eased within 48 hours. Once the swelling is gone, apply heat to speed up healing, help relieve pain, relax muscles and reduce joint stiffness.

- Use a heating pad set on low or medium. Or, use a hot-water bottle, heat pack or hot, damp towel wrapped around the injured area for moist heat. *[Note: Damp heat should be no warmer than 105°F.]*

- Apply heat to the injured area for 20 to 30 minutes, two to three times a day.

Liniments and balms also relieve the discomfort of sore muscles. They provide a cooling or warming sensation. Although these ointments only mask the pain of sore muscles and do nothing to promote healing, massaging them into the shoulder increases blood flow to help relax the muscles.

Treating Bursitis

Prolonged use of a joint or arthritis can cause the pain and discomfort of bursitis. Fortunately, these flare-ups can be controlled by:

- Applying ice packs to the sore shoulders.

- Taking a hot shower, applying a hot compress or heating pad to the affected shoulder, or rubbing the area with a deep-heating liniment.

Shoulder & Neck Pain, continued

Treating Neck Pain from Whiplash Injuries or Pinched Nerves

Always see a doctor anytime your motor vehicle is hit from the rear because the accident can cause a whiplash injury. The recommended treatment for whiplash injuries usually consists of using hot and cold packs, massage, exercises, sometimes a neck brace and pain-relieving medications such as aspirin, acetaminophen (Tylenol), ibuprofen (Motrin), and naproxen sodium (Aleve). Once your symptoms subside, you can resume normal activity.

After first checking with your doctor, you can ease neck discomfort by:

☐ Resting as much as possible by lying on your back.

☐ Using cold and hot packs. See how to use them in the previous section on treating tendinitis.

☐ Improving your posture. When sitting, select a chair with a straight back and push your buttocks into the chair's back. When standing, pull in your chin and stomach.

☐ Using a cervical (neck) pillow or roll a hand towel and place it under your neck.

☐ Avoiding activities that may aggravate your injuries.

☐ Covering your neck with a scarf if you venture out when the weather is cold.

☐ Practicing some of the stretching and strengthening exercises listed under the previous section on prevention.

Dealing with Arthritis and Osteoporosis

See the section on arthritis on page 98 and the section on osteoporosis on page 114 for information on these conditions.

⑲ Sinus Problems

A sinus infection feels like a bad cold. You get all these problems:

☐ Stuffy nose.

☐ Headache.

☐ Cough.

☐ Pressure inside your head.

☐ You can't sleep.

Your chances of getting a sinus infection increase if you:

☐ Have hay fever.

☐ Smoke.

☐ Have a nasal deformity.

☐ Have an abscess in an upper tooth.

☐ Sneeze hard with your mouth closed or blow your nose excessively when you have a cold.

Sinus complications can be serious. Your doctor can tell if you have a sinus infection with a physical exam, a laboratory study of a sampling of your nasal discharge and X-ray or CAT scan of the sinuses. You may need a prescription for an antibiotic and decongestant as well as a nasal spray and/or nose drops to clear the infection and reduce congestion. Severe cases may require surgery to drain the sinuses.

Questions To Ask

Do you have two or more of these problems?
- **A fever over 101°F.**
- **Greenish-yellow or bloody mucus.**
- **Severe headache which doesn't get better when you take aspirin, acetaminophen, ibuprofen or naproxen sodium.**
- **Headache that is worse in the morning or when bending forward.**
- **Pain between the nose and lower eyelid.**
- **A feeling of pressure inside the head.**
- **Eye pain, blurred vision or changes in vision.**
- **Cheek or upper jaw pain.**
- **Swollen face around eyes, nose, cheeks, forehead.**
- **Trouble sleeping or thinking clearly.**

YES  SEE DOCTOR

NO

 PROVIDE SELF-CARE

Sinus Problems, continued

Self-Care Procedures

A cool-mist humidifier can help. Super-moist air helps to make mucus thin. You can put a warm washcloth or warm compress over the sinus areas of your face. This can help with the pain. Other things that can help:

- [ ] Drink plenty of fluids to keep secretions thin and flowing.

- [ ] Take aspirin, acetaminophen, ibuprofen or naproxen sodium for pain. *[Note: Ask your doctor which ones are best for you.]*

- [ ] Use over-the-counter oral decongestants, but only if your doctor approves. *[Note: Older men who take ones that contain ephedrine or pseudoephedrine may experience urinary problems.]*

- [ ] You may also find it easier to take a combination over-the-counter product that contains both a pain reliever and a decongestant such as Tylenol Sinus, but only if your doctor approves.

- [ ] Be careful with nose drops. Don't use them for more than 3 days. If you use them longer, your sinuses can "forget" how to clear out. To avoid picking up germs, don't borrow nose drops from others. Don't let anyone else use yours. Throw the drops away after treatment.

⑳ Snoring

You've probably heard funny stories about snorers. Spouses sleep in separate beds or even separate bedrooms. Neighbors make them close their windows.

Well, snoring isn't so funny if you're the one who's left alone or if you have to put up with someone who snores. Nine out of ten snorers are men, and most of them are age 40 or over.

Snoring is the sound heard when the airway is blocked during sleep. It can result from a number of things: Obesity, enlarged tonsils and adenoids, deformities in the nasal passages, etc. Smoking, heavy drinking, overeating, especially before bedtime, and nasal allergies can lead to snoring by swelling the nasal passages and blocking the free flow of air. Also, persons who sleep on their backs are more likely to snore because the tongue falls back toward the throat and partly closes the airway.

Snoring can be merely a nuisance or can be a signal of a serious health problem, sleep apnea, which might even require surgery. Sleep apnea is a condition where breathing is stopped for a time period of at least 10 seconds, but usually 20 to 30 seconds or even up to 1 or 2 minutes during sleep. It is more common in men than in women and typically affects men who are middle-aged and older.

Sleep apnea can result from:

▢ An obstructed airway. This is more common as people age, especially those who are obese or who have smoked for many years.

▢ A central nervous system disorder such as a stroke, a brain tumor or even a viral brain infection.

▢ A chronic respiratory disease.

Questions to Ask

Has someone else noticed that breathing has stopped for 10 seconds or longer (sleep apnea) in the midst of snoring? **YES** → SEE DOCTOR

NO

cont'd on next page

Snoring, continued

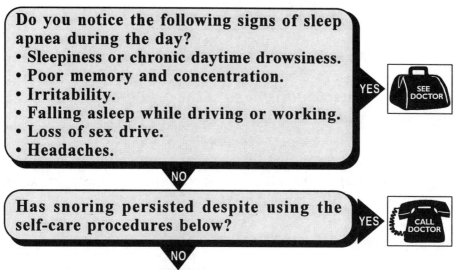

Do you notice the following signs of sleep apnea during the day?
• Sleepiness or chronic daytime drowsiness.
• Poor memory and concentration.
• Irritability.
• Falling asleep while driving or working.
• Loss of sex drive.
• Headaches.

YES → SEE DOCTOR

NO

Has snoring persisted despite using the self-care procedures below?

YES → CALL DOCTOR

NO

PROVIDE SELF-CARE

Self-Care Procedures

☐ Sleep on your side. Prop an extra pillow behind your back so you won't roll over. Try sleeping on a narrow sofa for a few nights to get accustomed to staying on your side.

☐ Sew a large marble or tennis ball into a pocket on the back of your pajamas. The discomfort it causes will remind you to sleep on your side.

☐ If you must sleep on your back, raise the head of the bed by putting bricks or blocks between the mattress and box springs. Or buy a wedge especially made for putting between the mattress and box spring to elevate the head section. Elevating the head can prevent the tongue from falling against the back of the throat, which can cause snoring.

☐ If you are heavy, lose weight. Excess fatty tissue in the throat can cause snoring.

☐ Don't drink alcohol or eat a heavy meal within 3 hours before bedtime. For some reason, both seem to foster snoring.

☐ If necessary, take a decongestant before retiring to relieve nasal congestion (which can also contribute to snoring). But check with your doctor before you do this if you have high blood pressure or heart disease.

☐ Get rid of allergens in the bedroom such as dust, down filled (feathered) pillows and bed linen. This may also relieve nasal congestion.

㉑ Sore Throat

Sore throats range from a mere scratch to pain so severe that even swallowing saliva is uncomfortable. Often, the cause of all this misery is a virus or bacteria. Viral sore throats are the more common of the two and don't respond to antibiotics; bacterial ones do. So it's important to know what kind of "bug" is roughing up your throat. A sore throat can result from a fungal infection too. In this case, an antifungal medicine is used to treat it.

Bacterial sore throats are most often caused by streptococcus (strep throat). Though uncommon in older persons, they bring a fever, headaches, or swollen, enlarged neck glands with them. Viral sore throats generally don't. But even doctors have trouble telling what "bug" causes a sore throat based on symptoms alone. So your doctor may take a throat culture.

If strep or other bacteria are the culprits, he or she will prescribe antibiotics. Be sure you finish taking all of the antibiotics. If left untreated, pneumonia, kidney inflammation, scarlet fever or rheumatic heart disease, could arise from a strep throat.

Questions To Ask

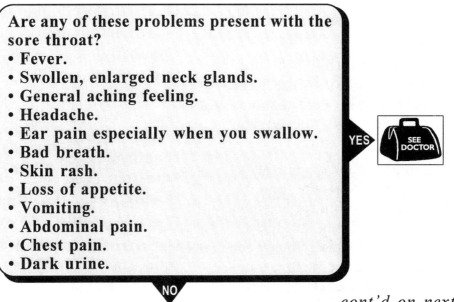

Are any of these problems present with the sore throat?
- **Fever.**
- **Swollen, enlarged neck glands.**
- **General aching feeling.**
- **Headache.**
- **Ear pain especially when you swallow.**
- **Bad breath.**
- **Skin rash.**
- **Loss of appetite.**
- **Vomiting.**
- **Abdominal pain.**
- **Chest pain.**
- **Dark urine.**

YES → SEE DOCTOR

NO

cont'd on next page

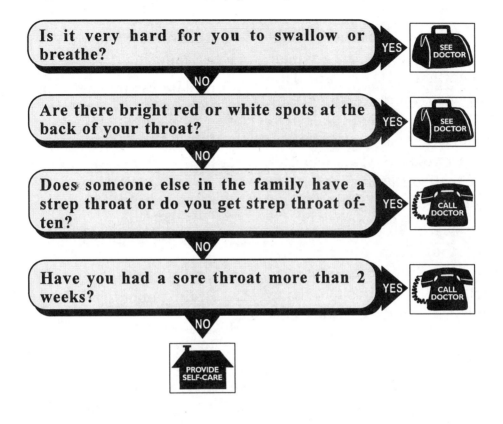

Self-Care Procedures

You can take some steps to relieve sore throat discomfort.

☐ Gargle every few hours with a solution of 1/2 teaspoon of salt dissolved in 4 ounces of warm water or with hot or cold double strength tea.

☐ Drink plenty of warm beverages, such as tea (with or without honey) and eat soup. Have reduced-sodium soup if you are on a sodium-restricted diet.

☐ Use a cool-mist vaporizer or humidifier in the room where you spend most of your time.

☐ Don't smoke. Smoke can aggravate sore throats and make it easier to get them.

☐ Avoid eating spicy foods.

☐ Suck on a piece of hard candy or medicated lozenge every so often.

☐ Take aspirin, acetaminophen, ibuprofen or naproxen sodium for the pain and for fever. *[Note: Ask your doctor which of these is right for you.]*

22 Tinnitus (Ringing in Ears)

Almost everyone experiences "ringing in the ears". It may last a minute or so, but then goes away. This doesn't mean there is something wrong. Imagine though, hearing a ringing noise in your ears and head, that doesn't go away. This maddening noise, called tinnitus, can range in volume from a ring to a roar.

It affects nearly 36 million Americans, most of them older adults. Seven million people are so seriously bothered by tinnitus that living a normal life is not possible. Tinnitus can, in fact, interfere with work, sleep, and normal communication with others.

Like a toothache, tinnitus isn't a disease in itself, but a symptom of another problem. Examples are:

- ☐ Ear wax blocking the ear canals.
- ☐ Food allergies.
- ☐ Reactions to medications such as aspirin.
- ☐ Middle-ear trauma or infections.
- ☐ Blood vessel abnormalities in the brain.
- ☐ Hair cell damage due to exposure to loud noise.
- ☐ Anemia.
- ☐ Meniere's disease.
- ☐ Diabetes.
- ☐ Brain tumors (rarely).

And sometimes, tinnitus is due simply to advancing age. It often accompanies loss of hearing. Occasionally, tinnitus is temporary and will not lead to deafness. Treatment is aimed at finding and treating the problem that causes the tinnitus.

Questions to Ask

Do you have severe pain in the ears, forehead or over the cheekbones, a severe headache, dizziness and/or sudden loss of hearing?

YES → SEEK EMERGENCY CARE

NO ↓

cont'd on next page

Tinnitus (Ringing in the Ears), continued

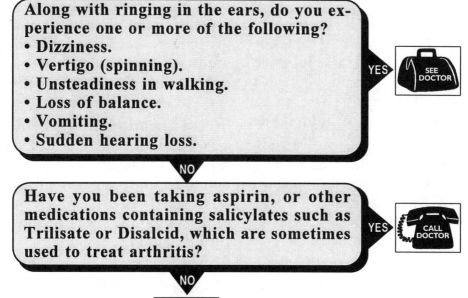

Along with ringing in the ears, do you experience one or more of the following?
- Dizziness.
- Vertigo (spinning).
- Unsteadiness in walking.
- Loss of balance.
- Vomiting.
- Sudden hearing loss.

YES → SEE DOCTOR

NO ↓

Have you been taking aspirin, or other medications containing salicylates such as Trilisate or Disalcid, which are sometimes used to treat arthritis?

YES → CALL DOCTOR

NO ↓

PROVIDE SELF-CARE

Self-Care Procedures

- For mild cases of tinnitus, play the radio or a white noise tape (white noise is a low, constant sound) in the background to help mask the tinnitus.

- Biofeedback or other relaxation techniques can help you calm down and concentrate, shifting your attention away from the tinnitus. Relaxation can reduce stress, which can aggravate tinnitus.

- Exercise regularly to promote good blood circulation.

- Ask your doctor or certified audiologist about a recently developed tinnitus masker, which looks like a hearing aid. Worn on the ear, it makes a subtle noise that masks the tinnitus without interfering with hearing and speech.

- If the noises started during or after traveling in an airplane, try pinching your nostrils and blowing through your nose. Chewing gum or sucking on hard candy may help prevent the ear popping and ringing sounds in the ear from happening when you do fly. Also, it is smart to avoid flying when you have an upper respiratory tract or ear infection.

- Limit your intake of caffeine, alcohol, nicotine and aspirin.

- Wear earplugs when exposed to loud noises to prevent damage to the ear.

23 Urinary Incontinence

If you have urinary incontinence, you suffer from a loss of bladder control or your body fails to store urine properly. As a result, you can't keep from passing urine, even though you may try to hold it in.

Urinary incontinence is not a normal part of aging, but often affects older persons because the sphincter muscles that open the bladder into the urethra become less efficient with aging.

You might feel embarrassed if you have urinary incontinence, but let your doctor know about it. It could be a symptom of a disorder that could lead to more trouble if not treated and, in most cases, the problem is curable and treatable.

Two categories of urinary incontinence are acute incontinence and persistent incontinence.

The acute form is generally a symptom of a new illness or condition, such as bladder infection, inflammation of the prostate, urethra, vagina, or from constipation.

Side effects of some medications such as water pills, tranquilizers and antihistamines can also result in acute urinary incontinence.

Acute urinary incontinence comes on suddenly. It is often easily reversed when the condition that caused it is treated.

Persistent incontinence comes on gradually over time. It lingers or remains, even after other conditions or illnesses have been treated. There are many types of persistent incontinence. The three types that account for 80% of cases are:

Stress Incontinence - Urine leaks out when there is a sudden rise in pressure in the abdomen (belly). The amount ranges from small leaks to large spills. This usually happens with coughing, sneezing, laughing, lifting, jumping, running or straining to have a bowel movement.

Stress incontinence is more common in women than in men.

Urge Incontinence - Inability to control the bladder when the urge to urinate occurs. This comes on suddenly so there is often not enough time to make it to the toilet. This type typically results in large accidents. It can be caused by a number of things, including an enlarged prostate gland, a spinal cord injury or illnesses such as multiple sclerosis and Parkinson's disease.

Mixed Incontinence - This type has elements of both stress and urge incontinence.

Other types of persistent incontinence are:

Overflow Incontinence - the constant dribbling of urine because the bladder overfills. This may be due to an enlarged prostate, diabetes or multiple sclerosis.

Urinary Incontinence, continued

Functional Incontinence - a person has trouble getting to the bathroom fast enough, even though he or she has bladder control. This can happen in a person who is physically challenged.

Total Incontinence - a rare type with complete loss of bladder control. Urine leakage can be continual.

Care and treatment for urinary incontinence will depend on the type and cause(s). The first step is to find out if there is an underlying problem and to correct it. Treatment can also include pelvic floor exercises, also called Kegel exercises, and other Self-Care Procedures (see page 83), medication, collagen injections (for a certain type of stress incontinence), or surgery to correct the specific problem.

Your primary doctor may evaluate and treat your incontinence or send you to a urologist, a doctor who specializes in treating problems of the bladder and urinary tract. Or, he or she may refer you to a geriatrician who specializes in the care and treatment of older adults.

Questions to Ask

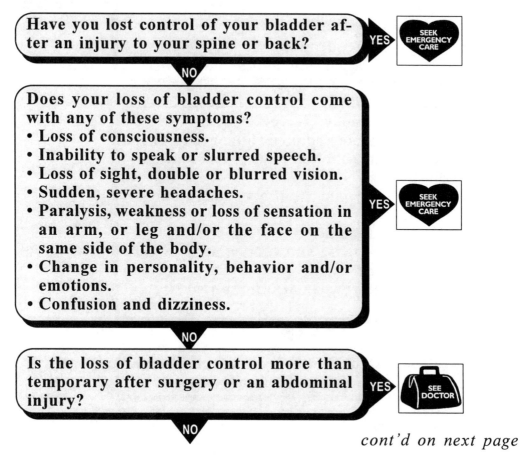

Have you lost control of your bladder after an injury to your spine or back? — YES → SEEK EMERGENCY CARE

NO

Does your loss of bladder control come with any of these symptoms?
- **Loss of consciousness.**
- **Inability to speak or slurred speech.**
- **Loss of sight, double or blurred vision.**
- **Sudden, severe headaches.**
- **Paralysis, weakness or loss of sensation in an arm, or leg and/or the face on the same side of the body.**
- **Change in personality, behavior and/or emotions.**
- **Confusion and dizziness.**

YES → SEEK EMERGENCY CARE

NO

Is the loss of bladder control more than temporary after surgery or an abdominal injury? — YES → SEE DOCTOR

NO

cont'd on next page

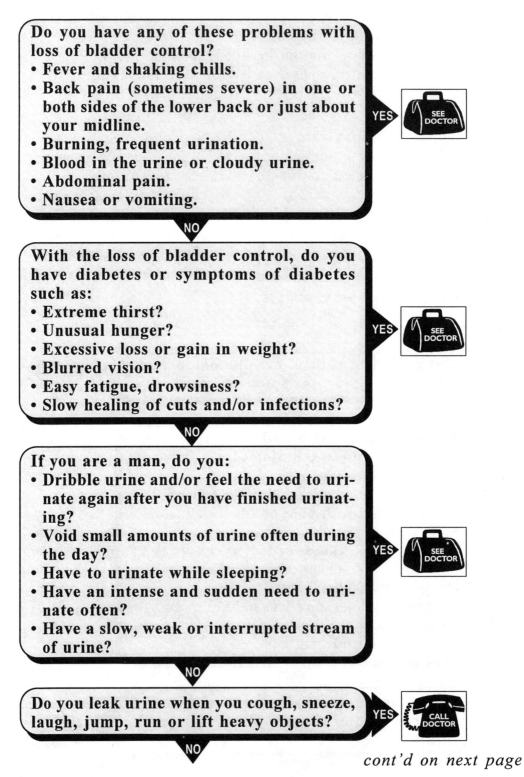

Do you have any of these problems with loss of bladder control?
- Fever and shaking chills.
- Back pain (sometimes severe) in one or both sides of the lower back or just about your midline.
- Burning, frequent urination.
- Blood in the urine or cloudy urine.
- Abdominal pain.
- Nausea or vomiting.

YES → SEE DOCTOR

NO ↓

With the loss of bladder control, do you have diabetes or symptoms of diabetes such as:
- Extreme thirst?
- Unusual hunger?
- Excessive loss or gain in weight?
- Blurred vision?
- Easy fatigue, drowsiness?
- Slow healing of cuts and/or infections?

YES → SEE DOCTOR

NO ↓

If you are a man, do you:
- Dribble urine and/or feel the need to urinate again after you have finished urinating?
- Void small amounts of urine often during the day?
- Have to urinate while sleeping?
- Have an intense and sudden need to urinate often?
- Have a slow, weak or interrupted stream of urine?

YES → SEE DOCTOR

NO ↓

Do you leak urine when you cough, sneeze, laugh, jump, run or lift heavy objects?

YES → CALL DOCTOR

NO ↓

cont'd on next page

Did you lose some bladder control only after taking a new medicine or after taking a higher dose of a medicine you were already taking? YES CALL DOCTOR

NO

 PROVIDE SELF-CARE

Self-Care Procedures

☐ Do Kegel exercises to strengthen your pelvic floor muscles. They can help treat or cure stress incontinence. Even elderly women who have leaked urine for years can benefit greatly from these exercises. Here's how to do them:

• First, identify where your pelvic floor muscles are. One way to do this is to start to urinate, then hold back and try to stop. If you can slow the stream of urine, even a little, you are using the right muscles. You should feel muscles squeezing around your urethra and anus.

• Next, relax your body, close your eyes and just imagine that you are going to urinate and then hold back from doing so. You should feel the muscles squeeze like you did in the step before this one.

• Squeeze the muscles for three seconds and then relax them for three seconds. When you squeeze and relax, count slowly. Start out doing this three times a day. Gradually work up to three sets of 10 contractions, holding each one for 10 seconds at a time. You can do them in lying, sitting and/or standing positions.

• Women can also use pelvic weights prescribed by their doctor. A women inserts a weighted cone into the vagina and squeezes the correct muscles to keep the weight from falling out.

☐ When you do these exercises:

• Do not tense the muscles in your belly or buttocks.

• Do not hold your breath, clench your fists or teeth or make a face.

• If you are not sure you're doing the exercise right, consult your doctor.

Urinary Incontinence, continued

- Squeeze your pelvic floor muscles right before and during whatever it is (coughing, sneezing, jumping, etc.) that causes you to lose urine. Relax the muscles once the activity is over.

- It may take several months to benefit from pelvic floor exercises and you have to keep doing them daily to maintain their benefit.

Other Self-Care Procedures:

☐ Avoid or limit drinks and medicines that have caffeine such as coffee, tea, colas, chocolate, No-Doz, etc.

☐ Limit carbonated drinks, alcohol, citrus juices, greasy and spicy foods and items that have artificial sweeteners. These can irritate the bladder.

☐ Drink one to two quarts of water throughout the day.

☐ Go to the bathroom often, even if you don't feel the urge. When you urinate, empty your bladder as much as you can. Relax for a minute or two and then try to go again. Keep a diary of when you have episodes of incontinence. If you find that you have accidents every 3 hours, for example, empty your bladder every 2-1/2 hours. Use an alarm clock or wristwatch with an alarm to remind you.

☐ Wear clothes you can remove quickly and easily when you use the bathroom. Examples are elastic-waist bottoms, and items with velcro closures or snaps instead of buttons and zippers. Also, look for belts that are easy to undo, or don't wear them.

☐ Wear absorbent pads or briefs such as Poise, Depends, Attends or similar drugstore brands.

☐ Ask your doctor if you would benefit from using self-catheters. A self-catheter is a clear, straw-like device, usually made of flexible plastic, that you insert into the opening of the urethra which helps you empty your bladder completely. Your doctor will need to show you how to use one. You need a prescription for self-catheters.

☐ To reduce the chances of accidents:

- Empty your bladder before you leave the house, take a nap and go to bed.

- Keep the pathway to your bathroom free of clutter and well lit. Make sure the bathroom door is left open until you use it.

- Use an elevated toilet seat and grab bars if these will make it easier for you to get on and off the toilet.

- Keep a bedpan, plastic urinal (for men) or portable commode chair near your bed. You can get these at medical supply stores and drug stores.

24 Urinary Tract Infection

About 1 out of 5 women will get a urinary tract infection (UTI) in her life. Some women gets lots of UTIs. Men get UTIs too, but not as often.

What is the urinary tract?

Your urinary tract is made up of these parts:

❑ Kidneys.

❑ Bladder.

❑ Ureters (tubes that connect the kidney to the bladder).

❑ Urethra (the tube that connects the bladder to the outside).

In most urinary tract infections, bacteria enter the urethra, travel to the bladder, multiply, and travel to other parts of the urinary tract, including the kidney. Bacteria can also reach the bladder from another part of the body through the blood stream.

In women, bacteria gain easy entry to the urethra as it is massaged during intercourse and can cause a bladder infection. Waiting too long to urinate after sexual intercourse will increase the chance of infection, because bacteria that enter the urethra have an opportunity to move farther up the urinary tract. Other things that increase the risk for UTIs:

❑ Any obstructions in the flow of urine like a kidney stone or enlarged prostate.

❑ Having a history of urinary tract infections.

❑ Having diabetes.

❑ Using a urinary catheter to empty the bladder.

❑ Urinary tract defects you were born with.

Sometimes, you don't even know you have a UTI. Most often though, you will have symptoms. They come on suddenly, with no warning. Here are some of the symptoms:

❑ A strong desire to urinate.

❑ Urinating more often than usual.

❑ A sharp pain or burning sensation in the urethra when you pass urine.

❑ Blood in the urine.

❑ Feeling like your bladder is still full after you pass urine.

❑ Soreness in the abdomen, back or sides.

❑ Chills, fever, nausea, and vomiting.

See a doctor if you have any of these symptoms. A UTI can be serious if you don't treat it. The doctor will test a sample of your

Urinary Tract Infection, continued

urine to find the problem. An antibiotic to treat the specific cause of the infection and pain relievers (if necessary) are the usual course of treatment.

Prevention

Here are some things you can do to keep from getting UTIs:

☐ If you're a woman, you should wipe from front to back after using the toilet to keep bacteria away from the urethral opening.

☐ Drink plenty of fluids to flush bacteria out of your system. Drink fruit juices, especially cranberry juices.

☐ Empty your bladder as soon as you feel the urge. Don't give bacteria chance to grow.

☐ Drink a glass of water before you have sex. Go to the bathroom before sex and as soon as you can after sex, even if you don't feel the urge.

☐ Use a water-soluble lubricant such as K-Y Jelly if you use a lubricant when you have sex.

☐ Wear cotton underwear. Bacteria like a warm, wet place. Cotton helps keep you cool and dry, because it lets air flow through it.

☐ Don't take bubble baths if you're prone to UTIs. Take showers instead of baths.

☐ Don't wear tight-fitting jeans, slacks, and undergarments.

☐ If you need to use a catheter to draw your own urine, make sure to wash your hands and clean the area around the urethra. Wash the catheter in soapy water after each use or use disposable ones. If you have a catheter that is kept in place, follow the instructions from your doctor for proper use and cleaning.

Urinary Tract Infection, continued

Questions To Ask

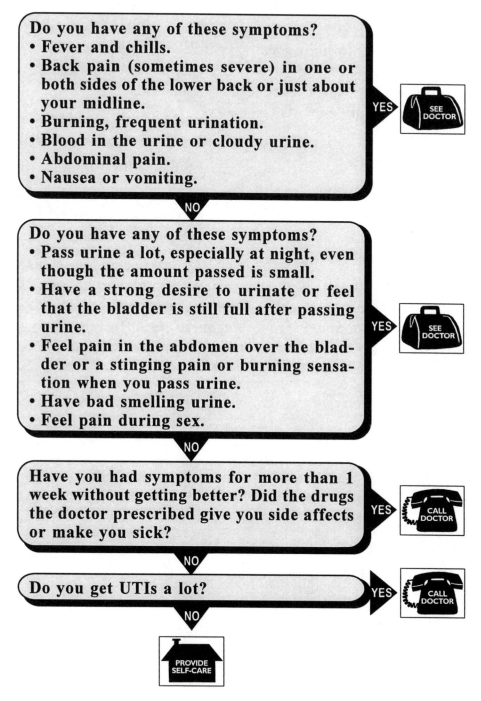

Do you have any of these symptoms?
- Fever and chills.
- Back pain (sometimes severe) in one or both sides of the lower back or just about your midline.
- Burning, frequent urination.
- Blood in the urine or cloudy urine.
- Abdominal pain.
- Nausea or vomiting.

YES → SEE DOCTOR

NO

Do you have any of these symptoms?
- Pass urine a lot, especially at night, even though the amount passed is small.
- Have a strong desire to urinate or feel that the bladder is still full after passing urine.
- Feel pain in the abdomen over the bladder or a stinging pain or burning sensation when you pass urine.
- Have bad smelling urine.
- Feel pain during sex.

YES → SEE DOCTOR

NO

Have you had symptoms for more than 1 week without getting better? Did the drugs the doctor prescribed give you side affects or make you sick?

YES → CALL DOCTOR

NO

Do you get UTIs a lot?

YES → CALL DOCTOR

NO

PROVIDE SELF-CARE

Urinary Tract Infection, continued

Self-Care Procedures

☐ Avoid alcohol, spicy foods, and coffee.

☐ Drink fluids often to help wash out the infection (at least 8 glasses including water every day). Cranberry juice is also a good choice.

☐ Get plenty of rest.

☐ Check for fever once in the morning and once in the afternoon or evening.

☐ Rest in bed if you have a high fever.

☐ Consult your pharmacist about a home test for urinary tract infections (Example: Biotel UTI). See your doctor if results show that you might have an infection.

☐ Urinate as soon as you feel the need to.

☐ Empty your bladder completely each time you pass urine.

☐ Empty your bladder after sex.

☐ Put off sexual intercourse until you have been free of symptoms for 2 weeks.

[Note: Urinary tract infections, when left untreated, can have serious consequences. If self-care procedures do not get rid of symptoms in three days, consult your doctor.]

㉕ Varicose Veins

Varicose veins are veins that are swollen, twisted and look blue and are close to the surface of the skin. They are unsightly and uncomfortable. Veins bulge, throb, and feel heavy. The legs and feet can swell. The skin can itch. Varicose veins may occur in almost any part of your body. They are most often seen in the back of the calf or on the inside of the leg between the groin and the ankle. Hemorrhoids (veins around the anus) can also become varicose.

Causes and risk factors for varicose veins include:

- ▭ Obesity.
- ▭ Past Pregnancies.
- ▭ Hormonal changes at menopause.
- ▭ Activities or hobbies that require standing positions for a long time.

- ▭ A family history of varicose veins.
- ▭ Past vein diseases such as thrombophlebitis (inflammation of a vein before a blood clot forms).

Medical treatment is not required for most varicose veins unless problems result, such as a deep-vein blood clot or severe bleeding which can be caused by injury to the vein.

Your doctor can take an X-ray of the vein (venogram) or an ultrasound to tell if there are any problems. Surgery can be done to remove enlarged veins. Sclerotherapy can also be done on smaller veins. This procedure uses a chemical injection into the vein that causes it to close up. Other veins then take over its work. Both of these treatments, however, may bring only temporary success, and more varicose veins can develop.

Questions to Ask

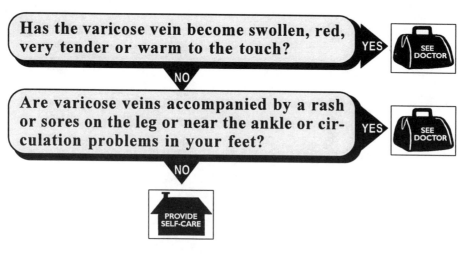

Has the varicose vein become swollen, red, very tender or warm to the touch? **YES** → SEE DOCTOR

NO ↓

Are varicose veins accompanied by a rash or sores on the leg or near the ankle or circulation problems in your feet? **YES** → SEE DOCTOR

NO ↓

PROVIDE SELF-CARE

Varicose Veins, continued

Self-Care Procedures

To relieve and prevent varicose veins:

☐ Don't cross your legs when sitting.

☐ Exercise regularly. Walking is a good choice. It improves leg and vein strength.

☐ Keep your weight down.

☐ Avoid standing for prolonged periods of time. If your job or hobby requires you to stand, shift your weight from one leg to the other every few minutes.

☐ Wear elastic support stockings.

☐ Don't wear clothing or undergarments that are tight or constrict your waist, groin or legs.

☐ Eat high-fiber foods like bran cereals, whole grain breads, fruits and vegetables to promote regularity. Constipation contributes to varicose veins.

☐ To prevent swelling, cut your salt intake.

☐ Exercise your legs. From a sitting position, rotate your feet at the ankles, turning them first clockwise, then counterclockwise, using a circular motion. Next, extend your legs forward and point your toes to the ceiling, then to the floor. Then, lift your feet off the floor and gently bend your legs back and forth at the knees.

☐ Elevate your legs when resting.

26 Vertigo

Occasionally, everyone experiences a little dizziness or wooziness. Looking overhead at moving clouds or watching the close-up scene of a car chase in a movie may suddenly leave you feeling dizzy and nauseated. Why? Because signals from your eyes and inner ear are mismatched. Your eyes are registering motion while your head and inner ear are standing still.

Vertigo, one type of dizziness, is caused by changes in the inner ear, the brain's gravity-and-motion detector. A viral or bacterial infection, or a blow to the head, can confuse the finely tuned balancing system of the inner ear and produce these unsettling feelings:

❑ Wooziness.

❑ Sense that room is spinning.

❑ Nausea.

❑ Blurred vision.

❑ Floating, rocking and/or rolling sensation.

❑ Sense of walking on an uneven surface.

Fortunately, few of vertigo's upsetting sensations are due to major illness.

Benign Positional Vertigo (BPV), the most common type of vertigo, occurs most often in middle aged people for no apparent reason. It may happen when you turn over in bed, get up, sit down, bend over or just tilt your head. The sensations start within seconds of changing position and last less than a minute. As bothersome as BPV is, it rarely signals more serious disease.

Meniere's disease also causes vertigo. Affecting mostly women between 30 and 60 years of age, Meniere's disease sometimes leads to permanent hearing loss. No one knows why people develop this condition, though the underlying causes may include spasms of blood vessels in the inner ear, fluid retention in the inner ear or allergic reactions. While attacks of Meniere's disease can continue for many years, some symptoms can be controlled by anti-nausea drugs, tranquilizers, antihistamines and/or diuretics (water pills).

Whereas dizziness significantly contributes to loss of balance and falls in the elderly, vertigo does not.

Prevention

Not all causes of vertigo are obvious. If you have occasional bouts of dizziness, try to avoid what brings it on:

❑ Alcohol. You don't have to be drunk to have alcohol interfere with your balance.

Vertigo, continued

- New medications, antibiotics or high doses of aspirin. Your dizziness may be drug-related if it begins shortly after taking them.

- Change in altitude. Less oxygen in the air at higher altitudes can cause dizziness in some people.

- Motion sickness. Low-level motion sickness can cause dizziness without nausea.

- Sudden movement. Avoid turning your head quickly or getting up suddenly.

- Fast moving objects. At the movies, look away from car chase scenes. And, don't look at moving clouds while you're standing still.

- Diseases such as diabetes and multiple sclerosis. People with diabetes should try to keep their blood sugar levels within normal range.

Questions to Ask

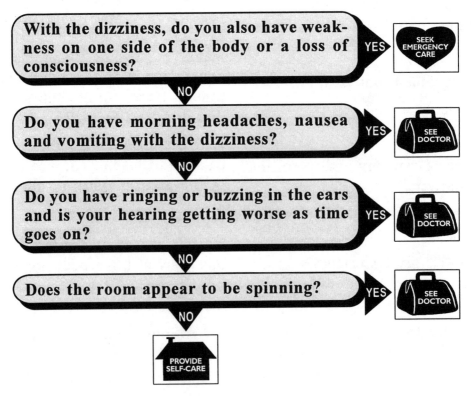

With the dizziness, do you also have weakness on one side of the body or a loss of consciousness? **YES** → SEEK EMERGENCY CARE

NO

Do you have morning headaches, nausea and vomiting with the dizziness? **YES** → SEE DOCTOR

NO

Do you have ringing or buzzing in the ears and is your hearing getting worse as time goes on? **YES** → SEE DOCTOR

NO

Does the room appear to be spinning? **YES** → SEE DOCTOR

NO

→ PROVIDE SELF-CARE

Vertigo, continued

Self-Care Procedures

After properly diagnosed, most cases of vertigo are easily treated in the doctor's office or at home. The following exercise is recommended for Benign Positional Vertigo (BPV).

- ☐ Sit on the side of the bed and lean to your right, resting the right ear on the bed. This might make you dizzy and nauseous at first.

- ☐ Wait 20 seconds until the dizziness stops and sit up straight.

- ☐ Wait another 20 seconds and repeat steps 1 and 2 on your left side.

- ☐ Do this exercise 10 to 15 times, three times a day.

For people diagnosed with Meniere's disease:

- ☐ Lie still in bed until the dizziness and nausea are gone.

- ☐ Do not walk without assistance.

- ☐ Avoid changing positions suddenly.

- ☐ Do not drive, climb ladders or work around dangerous machinery.

- ☐ Decrease the amount of salt and fluids in your diet.

- ☐ Avoid bright lights and do not read during attacks.

- ☐ Resume your normal activities when symptoms go away.

- ☐ Avoid alcohol, caffeine and tobacco. Doing so may reduce the frequency of attacks.

Major Medical Conditions

1. Alzheimer's Disease

Mysterious and frustrating, Alzheimer's afflicts nearly four million Americans, about 10 percent of the over 65 population, and perhaps as many as 45 percent of those 85 years or older. (In rare instances, Alzheimer's strikes earlier than 65.)

No one knows what causes Alzheimer's disease. Some research hints that a virus or infectious agent is the culprit. Others point to brain chemical deficits, a genetic predisposition and/or environmental toxins. Nevertheless, the end result is the death of brain cells that control intellect (the way your brain receives and processes information).

Signs and Symptoms

Alzheimer's Disease has a gradual onset. The signs and symptoms may progress in stages. How quickly they occur varies from person to person. The disease, does, however, eventually leave its victims totally unable to care for themselves.

Stage One
- ☐ Forgetfulness.
- ☐ Disorientation of time and place.
- ☐ Increasing inability to do routine tasks.
- ☐ Impairment in judgement.
- ☐ Lessening of initiative.
- ☐ Lack of spontaneity.
- ☐ Depression and fear.

Stage Two
- ☐ Increasing forgetfulness.
- ☐ Increasing disorientation.
- ☐ Wandering.
- ☐ Restlessness and agitation, especially at night.
- ☐ Repetitive actions.
- ☐ Muscle twitching and/or convulsive seizures may develop.

Stage Three
- ☐ Disorientation.
- ☐ Inability to recognize either themselves or other people.
- ☐ Speech impairment (may not be able to speak at all).
- ☐ Develop need to put everything into their mouths.
- ☐ Develop need to touch everything in sight.
- ☐ Become emaciated.

Alzheimer's, continued

☐ Complete loss of control of all body functions.

(Note: The stages very often overlap).

Treatment and Care

If someone you care about shows signs of Alzheimer's disease, see that they get medical attention to confirm (or rule out) the diagnosis. Not everything that looks like Alzheimer's is Alzheimer's. Brain tumors, blood clots in the brain, severe vitamin B12 deficiency, hypothyroidism, depression and some medicinal side effects can mimic Alzheimer's disease. (Unlike Alzheimer's, these problems may be treatable).

There is no known cure for Alzheimer's Disease. There is, however, a new Food and Drug Administration (FDA) approved medicine, tacrine, (Cognex), which appears to slow down the progression in some patients with mild to moderate Alzheimer's disease. Good planning and medical and social management are necessary to help both the victim and care-givers cope with the symptoms and maintain the quality of life for as long as possible. It's especially helpful to put structure in the life of someone who's in the early stages of Alzheimer's. Some suggestions include:

☐ Maintain daily routines.

☐ Post reminders on an oversized and prominently displayed calendar.

☐ Make "to do" lists of daily tasks for the person with Alzheimer's to complete, and ask him or her to check them off as they're completed.

☐ Put things in their proper places after use, to help the person with Alzheimer's find things when he or she needs them.

☐ Post safety reminders (like "turn off the stove") at appropriate places throughout the house.

☐ Also, see that the person with Alzheimer's eats well-balanced meals, goes for walks with family members, and otherwise continues to be as active as possible.

☐ Most medicinal therapies currently being used are experimental, except for the prescription medicine, Cognex, mentioned earlier. Also, medications are sometimes used to treat depression, paranoia and agitation, etc. These can minimize symptoms, but they will not necessarily improve memory.

At late stages, providing a safe environment is of utmost importance. Alzheimer's victims should wear identification bracelets or necklaces so they can be identified should they

95

Alzheimer's Disease, continued

be separated from their home environment. Seeking adult foster care or nursing home care for those who require supervision or medical management may be necessary.

Care-givers of Alzheimer's victims should also be given "care." They must deal with a number of financial, social, physical and emotional issues. Care for care-givers can be provided by professionals of home care, day care, respite care, service programs and self-help groups.

2. Angina

Angina is a common term shortened for the medical term "angina pectoris". The word angina itself means pain; pectoris means chest. Angina is the chest pain or discomfort brought on by decreased circulation in the heart and heart muscle itself. It results from a shortage of oxygen and other nutrients to any part of the heart muscle.

Signs and Symptoms

☐ Squeezing pressure, heaviness, or mild ache in the chest (usually behind the breastbone).

☐ Aching in a tooth accompanied by this squeezing pressure or heaviness in the chest.

☐ Aching into the neck muscles or jaw.

☐ Aching into one or both arms in whole or in part.

☐ Aching into the back.

☐ A feeling of gas in the upper abdomen and lower chest.

☐ A feeling that you're choking.

☐ Paleness and sweating.

These symptoms may not be extreme so are often neglected. It is better for you to report an episode of angina to your doctor, than not to do so, even if you might feel foolish if something minor is the cause.

Episodes of angina are usually associated with:

☐ Anger or excitement.

☐ Emotional shock.

☐ Physical work in which the discomfort goes away when the work is stopped.

☐ Waking up at night with discomfort.

☐ Arm use.

In all of these situations, there is relief from the distress when the activity is stopped.

Many people who experience angina for the first time fear they're having a heart attack. Here's why angina and heart attack are mistaken for each other:

Angina, continued

- [ ] Both can be caused by a buildup of fatty plaque (atherosclerosis) in the heart arteries (coronary arteries). These plaques cause a decrease in flow to the heart muscle beyond the partial obstruction.

- [ ] In both, the pain is felt in the chest and may spread to both arms, shoulders, or neck.

- [ ] Both may be brought on by physical exertion.

- [ ] Both are most prevalent in men who are 50 and older and women who are past menopause.

But a heart attack and angina have differences too:

- [ ] A heart attack results in a damaged or injured heart muscle, angina does not. Rather, anginal pain is a warning sign of a potential heart attack. The pain indicates that the heart muscle isn't getting enough blood.

- [ ] Rest or nitroglycerin relieves angina, but not a heart attack.

A doctor can generally diagnose angina as stable or unstable, based on your description of the painful episode, but he or she many need to confirm it with a stress test (a measurement of heart function taken while you exercise on a treadmill). Unstable angina, a symptom of coronary artery disease, requires immediate attention. This serious medical condition affects many Americans, some of whom may not know they have heart disease. Although unstable angina can be a precursor to heart attack, prompt treatment can lower the risk of death or serious cardiac events.

Factors like high blood pressure, obesity, diabetes, high cholesterol, smoking, or a family history of atherosclerotic heart disease increase the odds of getting angina.

Treatment and Care

- [ ] Consult your physician or a cardiologist who should insist on appropriate studies to diagnose your condition, therapy to treat it, and close follow-up. The keystones to treatment are:

- [ ] Appropriate medicine(s) such as one(s) to control high blood pressure; nitroglycerin or other medication to temporarily dilate or widen the coronary arteries which ease blood flow to the heart. Nitroglycerin takes effect within a few minutes.

- [ ] Daily physical exercise for endurance, preferably prescribed just for you by an exercise physiologist to whom a cardiologist has referred you (exercise must be maintained below the onset of any discomfort. It may not be applicable at all for some individuals).

Angina, continued

- [ ] Don't smoke. Nicotine in cigarettes constricts the arteries and prevents proper blood flow.

- [ ] Avoid large, heavy meals. Instead, eat lighter meals throughout the day.

- [ ] Rest after eating, or engage in some quiet activity.

- [ ] Minimize exposure to cold, windy weather.

- [ ] Lower your cholesterol level if it's high, by following your doctor's advice.

- [ ] Avoid sudden engagement in rather severe exercise or other physical stress.

- [ ] Avoid anger and frustration whenever possible.

3. Arthritis

Arthritis robs some 40 million Americans of their freedom of movement by breaking down the protective cartilage in the joints. By destroying cartilage, arthritis results in pain and decreased movement.

Many forms of arthritis exist. Three of the most common are osteoarthritis, rheumatoid arthritis, and ankylosing spondylitis.

Osteoarthritis is a painful degeneration of the cartilage in the weight-bearing and frequently used joints. As far as researchers can tell, this kind of arthritis is typically brought on by genetics, activity, and wear and tear on the joints. Osteoarthritis usually affects older people and is the most common type of arthritis.

Rheumatoid arthritis (RA) is caused by a chronic inflammation of the fingers, wrists, ankles, elbows, and/or knees, causing pain, swelling, and tenderness. Morning stiffness lasting longer than an hour is very common. RA affects women more often than men. It usually begins between age thirty and forty and continues with aging. At present, it is not curable.

Ankylosing spondylitis generally begins in young men between the ages of 15 and 45 and is characterized by a stiff backbone, accompanied by low back pain. The arthritis can spread to other places, such as the hips, the ribs, and the jaw.

Signs and Symptoms

Symptoms of arthritis, therefore, depend upon the type of arthritis that is present. Symptoms generally include:

- [ ] Stiffness.

- [ ] Swelling in one or more joints.

- [ ] Deep, aching pain in a joint.

- [ ] Any pain associated with movement of a joint.

Arthritis, continued

☐ Tenderness or warmth, in afflicted joints.

☐ Fever, weight loss, or fatigue that accompanies joint pain.

Treatment and Care

If your doctor does diagnose arthritis, he or she may prescribe medication (usually aspirin or a non-steroidal anti-inflammatory medicine), rest, heat or cold treatment, and some physical therapy or exercise, depending on what kind of arthritis you have. The goal is to reduce pain and improve joint mobility.

Among those treatments, perhaps exercise is the most important, whether it be some form of stretching, isometrics, or simple endurance exercise. Low-impact exercise seems to provide both physical relief and psychological benefits. For example, it prevents the muscles from shrinking, while inactivity encourages both loss of muscle tone and bone deterioration. Too much exercise, however, will cause more pain in those with rheumatoid arthritis or osteoarthritis. So if you have arthritis, consult your physician, a physical therapist, or a physiatrist (a doctor who specializes in rehabilitative treatment) to assist you in developing an exercise program.

One form of exercise that's effective and soothing is hydrotherapy, or movement done in water. It allows freedom of movement and puts less stress on the joints because nearly all of the body weight is supported by the water. Doctors highly recommend swimming, too.

But remember, hydrotherapy, or any form of exercise, should never produce pain. One message that can't be emphasized enough is "Go easy". If you begin to hurt, stop and rest or apply ice packs.

The following exercise suggestions may provide relief:

☐ Choose exercise routines that use all affected joints.

☐ Keep movements gradual, slow, and gentle.

☐ If a joint is inflamed, don't exercise it.

☐ Don't overdo it. Allow yourself sufficient rest.

☐ Concentrate on freedom of movement, especially in the water, and be patient.

4. Cancer

Cancer refers to a broad group of diseases in which body cells grow out of control and are or become malignant (harmful).

Cancer is the second leading cause of death in the United States (heart disease is first). Current estimates say that 30 percent of all Americans

Cancer, continued

will develop some kind of cancer in their lifetimes. The most common forms are cancer of the skin, lungs, colon and rectum, breast, prostate, urinary tract, and uterus.

Exactly what causes all cancers has not yet been found. Evidence suggests, however, that cancer could result from complex interactions of viruses, a person's genetic make-up, their immune status and their exposure to other risk factors that may promote cancer. These include:

❑ Exposure to: The sun's ultraviolet rays, nuclear radiation, X-rays, and radon.

❑ Use of tobacco or alcohol for some cancers.

❑ Use of certain medicines such as DES (a synthetic estrogen).

❑ Polluted air and water.

❑ Dietary factors such as a high fat diet, specific food preservatives, namely nitrates and nitrites; char-broiling and char-grilling meats.

❑ Exposure to a variety of chemicals such as asbestos, benzenes, VC (vinyl chloride), wood dust, some ingredients of cigarette smoke, etc).

Signs and Symptoms

Symptoms of cancer depend on the type of cancer, the stage that it is in and whether or not it has spread to other parts of the body (metasta-sis). The following signs and symptoms should always be brought to your doctor's attention because they could be warning signals of cancer:

❑ Any change in bladder or bowel habits.

❑ A lump or thickening in the breast, testicles or anywhere else.

❑ Unusual vaginal bleeding or rectal discharge or any unusual bleeding.

❑ Persistent hoarseness or nagging cough.

❑ A sore throat that won't go away.

❑ Noticeable change in a wart or mole.

❑ Indigestion or difficulty swallowing.

Treatment and Care

Cancer is not necessarily fatal and is, in many cases, curable. Early detection and proper treatment increase your chances for surviving cancer. Early detection is more likely if you:

❑ Know the above warning signs for cancer and report any of these warning signs to your doctor if they occur.

❑ Do regular self-examination such as monthly breast self-examination if you are a woman, (see page 17) and a monthly testicular self-exam if you are a man.

Cancer, continued

☐ Look at yourself in the mirror for any noticeable changes in warts or moles or for any wounds that have not healed.

☐ Ask your doctor to perform routine tests such as pap tests, breast exams, mammograms, if you are a woman, and Prostate Specific Antigen (PSA) blood test, along with a digital rectal exam after age 50 if you are a man. Other tests include one for colorectal abnormalities (sigmoidoscopy) and one to check for blood in the stools. *[Note: Though uncommon, men can also get breast cancer. Men should ask their doctor for signs to look for.]*

If and when cancer is diagnosed, treatment will depend on the type of cancer present, the stage it is in, and your body's response to treatment.

Cancer treatment generally includes one or more of the following:

☐ Surgery to remove the cancerous tumor(s) and clear any obstruction to vital passageways caused by the cancer.

☐ Radiation therapy.

☐ Chemotherapy.

☐ Possibly immunotherapy.

Prevention

Moreover, measures can be taken to lower the risk for certain forms of cancer:

Dietary Measures:

☐ Reduce the intake of total dietary fat to no more than 30% of total calories and reduce the intake of saturated fat to less than 10% of total calories.

☐ Eat more fruits, vegetables, and whole grains, especially:

• Broccoli and other cabbage family vegetables including cabbage and brussel sprouts. These contain sulforaphane, a cancer-fighting chemical and antioxidant.

• Deep yellow-orange fruits and vegetables such as canteloupe, peaches, tomatoes, carrots, sweet potatoes, squash and very dark green vegetables like spinach, greens and broccoli for their beta-carotene content.

• Strawberries, citrus fruits, broccoli and green peppers for vitamin C.

• Whole grain breads, cereals, fresh fruits and vegetables and legumes for their dietary fiber content.

☐ Consume salt-cured, salt-pickled, and smoked foods only in moderation.

☐ Drink alcoholic beverages only in moderation, if at all.

Cancer, continued

Lifestyle Measures:

☐ Do not smoke, use tobacco products or inhale second hand smoke.

☐ Limit your exposure to known carcinogens such as asbestos, radon, and other workplace chemicals as well as pesticides and herbicides.

☐ Have X-rays only when necessary.

☐ Limit your exposure to the sun's ultraviolet (UV) rays, sun lamps and tanning booths. Protect your skin from the sun's UV rays with sunscreen, applied frequently and containing a sun protection factor (SPF) of 15 or higher, and protective clothing (sun hats, long sleeves, etc.).

☐ Reduce stress. Emotional stress may weaken the immune system that is relied on to fight off stray cancer cells.

5. Cataracts

A cataract is a cloudy area in the lens or lens capsule of the eye. A cataract blocks or distorts light entering the eye. This causes problems with glare from lamps or the sun and vision gradually becomes dull and fuzzy, even in daylight. Most of the time, cataracts occur in both eyes, but only one eye may be affected. If they form in both eyes, one eye can be worse than the other, because each cataract develops at a different rate. During the time cataracts are forming, vision can be helped with frequent eyeglass changes.

There are several causes of cataracts:

Senile cataracts are the most common form. Cataracts can accompany aging, probably due to changes in the chemical state of lens proteins. About half of Americans, ages 65 to 74 have cataracts. About 70 percent of those over 75 have this condition.

Traumatic cataracts develop after a foreign body enters the lens capsule with enough force to cause specific damage.

Complicated cataracts occur secondary to other diseases such as diabetes mellitus, hypothyroidism, or other eye disorders such as detached retinas, glaucoma, retinitis pigmentosa, etc. Ionizing radiation or infrared rays can also lead to this type of cataracts.

Toxic cataracts can result from medicine or chemical toxicity. Smokers have an increased risk for developing cataracts.

Signs and Symptoms

☐ Cloudy, fuzzy, foggy or filmy vision.

☐ Sensitivity to light and glazed nighttime vision. This can cause

Cataracts, continued

problems when driving at night because headlights seem too bright.

☐ Double vision.

☐ Pupils which are normally black appear milky white.

☐ Halos may appear around lights.

☐ Changes in the way you see colors.

☐ Problems with glare from lamps or the sun.

☐ Better vision for awhile, only in farsighted people. This is called "second sight".

Prevention

☐ Limit exposing your eyes to X-rays, microwaves and infrared radiation.

☐ Use sunglasses that block ultraviolet (UV) light.

☐ Wear a wide-brimmed or baseball style hat to keep direct sunlight from your eyes while outdoors.

☐ Avoid overexposure to sunlight.

☐ Wear glasses or goggles that protect your eyes whenever you use strong chemicals, power tools or other instruments that could result in eye injury.

☐ Don't smoke.

☐ Avoid heavy drinking.

☐ Foods high in beta-carotene and/or vitamin C may help to prevent or delay cataracts. Eat them often. Examples include: Carrots, cantaloupes, oranges, and broccoli.

☐ Follow your doctor's advice to keep other illnesses such as diabetes and hypothyroidism under control.

Treatment and Care

If the vision loss caused by a cataract is only slight, surgery may not be needed. A change in your glasses, stronger bifocals, or the use of magnifying lenses, and taking measure to reduce glare may help improve your vision and be enough for treatment. To reduce glare, wear sunglasses that filter UV light when you are outdoors. When indoors, make sure your lighting is not too bright or pointed directly at you. Use soft, white light bulbs instead of clear ones, for example, and arrange to have light reflect off walls and ceilings. When cataracts interfere with your life, however, surgery should be considered.

Modern cataract surgery is safe and effective in restoring vision. Ninety-five percent of operations are successful. For the most part, surgery can be done on an outpatient basis or as part of an overnight hospital stay.

A person who has cataract surgery usually gets an artificial lens at the same time. A plastic disc called an intraocular lens, is placed in the lens capsule inside the eye. Other choices are contact lenses and cataract glasses. Your doctor will help you to decide which choice is best for you.

It takes a couple of months for an eye to heal after cataract surgery. Experts say it is best to wait until your first eye heals before you have surgery on the second eye if it, too, has a cataract.

Following surgery, continue to protect your eyes from ultraviolet light by wearing UV-filtering sunglasses.

6. Chronic Obstructive Pulmonary Disease (COPD)

Can you imagine what it would feel like to breathe with a plastic bag over your head? That's exactly what emphysema feels like.

Emphysema is often accompanied by chronic bronchitis. Together, they are referred to as "chronic obstructive pulmonary disease", (COPD).

Millions of Americans are forced to lead restricted lives because they have this chronic lung condition.

With emphysema, the air sacs (alveoli) in the lungs are destroyed, and the lung loses its elasticity, along with its ability to take in oxygen. Genetic factors are responsible for 3 to 5 percent of all cases of emphysema, and occupational and environmental exposure to irritants can also cause the disease. But the vast majority of people with emphysema are cigarette smokers aged 50 or older. In fact, emphysema is sometimes called the smoker's disease because of its strong link with cigarettes.

Cigarette smoking is also the most common cause of chronic bronchitis. Other culprits include allergens and air pollution. These lead to repeated irritation or infection in the bronchial tubes, (the passageways for air moving to and from the lungs). Chronic bronchitis results in abnormal air exchange in the lung and causes permanent damage to the respiratory tract.

Persons with chronic bronchitis have a cough that brings up a lot of phlegm for as long as three months or more, for more than two years in a row when no other condition exists to cause this.

Signs of Emphysema
Emphysema takes a number of years to develop, and early symptoms can

Chronic Obstructive Pulmonary Disease (COPD), continued

be easily missed. Symptoms to look out for include:

- [ ] Breathing through pursed lips.
- [ ] Shortness of breath on exertion.
- [ ] Wheezing.
- [ ] Fatigue.
- [ ] Slight body build with marked weight loss and barrel chest.

Signs of Chronic Bronchitis:

- [ ] A cough that is productive, i.e., one that produces mucus or phlegm.
- [ ] Shortness of breath upon exertion (in early stages).
- [ ] Shortness of breath at rest (in later stages).

Treatment and Care

A doctor can diagnose emphysema based on your medical history, a physical exam, a chest X-ray, and a lung function test (spirometry). The diagnoses for chronic bronchitis can be made by medical history alone. By the time emphysema is detected, though, anywhere from 50 to 70 percent of your lung tissue may already be destroyed. Your doctor may recommend the following for COPD:

- [ ] A program to help you stop smoking.
- [ ] Avoiding second hand smoke.
- [ ] Avoiding dust, fumes, pollutants, and other irritating inhalants.
- [ ] Physical therapy to help loosen mucus in your lungs.
- [ ] Using cough medicines with an expectorant.
- [ ] Avoiding exposure to cold, wet weather.
- [ ] Air conditioning, a medically approved air purifiers, or a cool-mist vaporizer.
- [ ] Daily exercise.
- [ ] A diet that includes adequate amounts of all essential nutrients.
- [ ] Prescription medication which may include a bronchodilator, steroids, and antibiotics (to fight a bacterial infection or prevent one).
- [ ] Annual flu vaccinations.
- [ ] A pneumonia vaccination given once as recommended by your doctor.
- [ ] Supplemental oxygen.
- [ ] COPD is not reversible, however, so prevention is the only real way to avoid permanent damage.

7. Coronary Heart Disease

The coronary arteries supply blood to the heart muscle. When they became narrowed or blocked, usually by fatty deposits and or blood clots, the heart muscle can be damaged. This is coronary heart disease.

Two conditions of coronary heart disease are "angina pectoris" (see angina on page 96), and acute myocardial infarction (heart attacks). Every day, about 4,000 Americans have heart attacks, one every 20 seconds. And each year, nearly 600,000 people die of coronary artery disease, making it the nation's number one killer.

Fortunately, heart disease claims fewer and fewer lives each year, thanks to advances in medical treatment of heart disease and growing public awareness of the benefits of exercise and good nutrition. Prevention is of utmost importance.

Prevention

To avoid coronary heart disease, the American Heart Association suggests the following steps:

☐ Have your blood pressure checked regularly. High blood pressure can increase the risk for atherosclerosis. To control high blood pressure, follow your doctor's advice. You may be told to reduce your intake of salt if you are "salt sensitive". Salt sensitive means eating too much salt can raise your blood pressure and reducing salt can help lower it.

☐ If you smoke, quit. Nicotine constricts blood flow to the heart, decreases oxygen supply to the heart, and seems to play a significant role in the development of coronary artery disease.

☐ Ask your doctor to check you for diabetes, which is associated with atherosclerosis. Follow his or her advice if you have diabetes.

☐ Maintain a normal body weight. People who are obese are more prone to atherosclerosis, high blood pressure, and diabetes, and therefore coronary heart disease.

☐ Follow a diet low in saturated fat and cholesterol. Saturated fats are found in meats, dairy products with fat, hydrogenated vegetable oils and some tropical oils, like coconut and palm kernel oils. High-saturated fat, high-cholesterol diets contribute to the fatty sludge that accumulates inside artery walls.

☐ Get some form of aerobic exercise at least three times a week for 20 minutes at a time. Sitting around hour after hour, day after day, week in and week out with no regular physical activity

Coronary Heart Disease, continued

may cause circulation problems later in life and contribute to atherosclerosis. Consult your doctor before starting any new exercise program. A treadmill stress test may need to be done before engaging in aerobic exercise.

☐ Reduce the harmful effects of stress by practicing relaxation techniques and improving your outlook on daily events. Stress has been linked to elevated blood pressure, among other health problems.

☐ Get regular medical check-ups.

Know the signs of a heart attack so you can get immediate medical attention if necessary, before it's too late. They are:

☐ Chest discomfort or pressure lasting several minutes or longer.

☐ Discomfort or pressure that spreads to the shoulder, neck, arm, and/or jaw.

☐ Nausea or vomiting associated with chest pain.

☐ A cold sweat.

☐ Difficult breathing.

☐ Faintness or dizziness.

☐ Stomach upset.

☐ A sense of impending disaster.

Treatment and Care

If you think you're having a heart attack, get to a hospital as quickly as possible. A clot dissolving injection can reduce the risk of mortality and severity of damage to the heart muscle if given within four hours. Emergency surgery such as angioplasty can also prevent damage to the heart muscle. With this surgery, a balloon-tipped catheter is inserted into the blocked or narrowed heart vessel(s). The balloon is inflated and deflated a few times to open up the narrowed part. It is then withdrawn.

Care following a heart attack will depend on the amount of damage done to the heart muscle which can be assessed by specific medical tests and procedures. Your doctor will determine the course of treatment. This could include any or many of the following:

☐ Medication (cardiac, blood pressure, cholesterol lowering medicines, etc).

☐ Hospitalization for treatment and recovery from the heart attack.

☐ Cardiac rehabilitation for lifestyle changes including: Smoking cessation, weight loss, low-fat, cholesterol-controlling diet, behavior modification, stress management relaxation techniques.

Coronary Heart Disease, continued

☐ Surgery if indicated such as balloon angioplasty or coronary artery bypass grafts.

☐ Long-term maintenance and medical follow-up.

8. Diabetes

Diabetes is a condition which results when a person's body doesn't make any insulin, enough insulin or doesn't use insulin the right way. Insulin is a hormone made in the pancreas gland that helps your cells use blood sugar for energy. When insulin is in short supply, the glucose (sugar) in the blood can become dangerously high. That's why someone who is diabetic may have to take insulin by injection, or pills by mouth which help the body secrete more of its own insulin or make better use of the insulin it does secrete. Some diabetics, however, require no medication. All persons with diabetes must follow a controlled diet and exercise regularly to prevent their blood sugar from getting too high.

There are two (2) forms of diabetes:

Type 1 - (sometimes called insulin-dependent diabetes mellitus (IDDM) or juvenile diabetes) is more severe and usually shows up before the age of 30, but may occur at any age. Insulin injections are essential as well as dietary control and exercise.

Type 2 - (sometimes called non-insulin dependent diabetes mellitus (NIDDM) or adult-onset diabetes) is less severe, usually affecting persons who are 40 years of age or older and overweight. This type is most often treated with diet and exercise and sometimes oral medicine. Occasional insulin injections may be required as well.

Diabetes can contribute to hardening of the arteries, strokes, kidney failure, blindness, and gangrene.

Signs and Symptoms
The American Diabetes Association uses the acronyms DIABETES and CAUTION to help identify the warning signs of diabetes.

☐ **Drowsiness.**

☐ **Itching.**

☐ **A family history of diabetes.**

☐ **Blurred vision.**

☐ **Excessive weight.**

☐ **Tingling, numbness, or pain in extremities.**

☐ **Easy fatigue.**

☐ **Skin infection, slow healing of cuts and scratches, especially on the feet.**

Diabetes, continued

Other signs are:

- ☐ Constant or frequent urination.
- ☐ Abnormal thirst.
- ☐ Unusual hunger.
- ☐ The rapid loss of weight.
- ☐ Irritability.
- ☐ Obvious weakness and fatigue.
- ☐ Nausea and vomiting.

You don't necessarily have to experience all of these warning signs to be diabetic; only one or two may be present. Some people show no warning signs whatsoever and find out they're diabetic after a routine blood test. If you have a family history of diabetes, you should have a blood sugar test at least once a year. Being overweight increases your risk significantly. A diet high in sugar and low in fiber may increase your risk if you are prone to developing diabetes. Pregnancy can trigger diabetes in some women.

Treatment and Care

Treatment for diabetes will depend on the type and severity of the disorder. Both forms, however, require a treatment plan that maintains normal, steady blood sugar levels. This can be accomplished by:

- ☐ Proper dietary measures that give prescribed amounts of protein, fat, and carbohydrates, set up in regular meals and are low in simple sugars, adequate in dietary fiber, and that promote weight reduction if necessary.
- ☐ Exercise.
- ☐ Medicine - Oral pills or insulin shots, if necessary.

With either type of diabetes, routine care and follow up treatment is important. Careful control of blood sugar levels can allow a person with diabetes to lead a normal, productive life. Persons who are genetically predisposed to diabetes should watch their weight, control their eating habits, and exercise regularly to reduce their risk of getting the disease.

9. Diverticulosis and Diverticulitis

No one is sure why, but sometimes small sac-like pockets protrude from the wall of the colon. This is called diverticulosis. Increased pressure within the intestines seems to be responsible. The pockets, called diverticuli, can fill with intestinal waste.

Sometimes, though, the intestinal pouches become inflamed, in which case the condition is called diverticulitis.

Diverticulosis and Diverticulitis, continued

Many older persons have diverticulosis. The digestive system becomes sluggish as a person ages. Things that increase the risk for diverticulosis include:

- Not eating enough dietary fiber. Diverticulosis is common in nations where fiber intake is low.

- Continual use of medicines that slow bowel action. (Example: Painkillers, anti-depressants)

- Overuse of laxatives.

- Having family members who have diverticulosis.

- Having coronary heart or gall-bladder disease.

- Being obese.

Signs and Symptoms

In most cases, diverticulosis causes no discomfort. When there are symptoms they are usually:

- Tenderness, mild cramping or a bloated feeling usually on the lower left side of the abdomen

- Sometimes constipation or diarrhea

- Occasionally bright red blood in the stools

With diverticulitis, you can experience:

- Severe, constant and disabling pain in the abdomen.

- Nausea.

- Fever.

The pain felt is made worse with a bowel movement. If these things occur, you should see your doctor.

Treatment and Care

Diverticular disease can't be cured, but you can reduce the discomfort, and prevent complications. Follow a diet high in fiber throughout life. You can add more fiber to your diet with fresh fruits, vegetables, and whole-grain foods. Check with your doctor about adding wheat bran to your diet. These pass through the system quickly, decreasing pressure in the intestines. Do, however, avoid corn, seeds, and foods with seeds like figs, breads or buns with seeds, etc. Seeds are easily trapped in the troublesome pouches.

You should also drink 1½ to 2 quarts of water every day. Avoid the regular use of laxatives that make your bowel muscles contract such as Ex-Lax. In fact, you should consult your doctor before taking any laxatives. If you are not able to eat a high-fiber diet, ask your doctor about taking bulk-producing laxatives like Metamucil. These are not habit-forming. Try, too, not to strain when you have bowel movements. Finally, get regular exercise.

Diverticulosis and Diverticulitis, continued

If you have diverticulitis, your doctor may prescribe:

- ☐ Antibiotics.
- ☐ Other medicines to reduce spasms in the colon.
- ☐ Bed rest until you improve.

10. Glaucoma

Glaucoma happens when the pressure of the liquid in the eye gets too high and causes damage.

It tends to run in families and is one of the most common major eye disorders in people above the age of 60. The risk of getting glaucoma increases with age. It can also be triggered or aggravated by some medicines like antihistamines and antispasmodics.

Signs and Symptoms

There are two types of glaucoma:

- ☐ Chronic or open-angle glaucoma. This type takes place gradually and usually causes no pain and no symptoms early on. When signs and symptoms begin they include:
  - Loss of side (peripheral) vision.
  - Blurred vision.

In the late stages, symptoms include:

- Vision loss in larger areas (side and central vision) usually in both eyes.
- Blind spots.
- Seeing halos around lights.
- Poor night vision.
- Blindness if not treated early enough.

- ☐ Acute or angle-closure glaucoma. This type can occur suddenly. It is a medical emergency!

Signs and symptoms include:

- Severe pain in and above the eye.
- Severe throbbing headache.
- Fogginess of vision, halos around lights.
- Redness in the eye, swollen upper eyelid.
- Dilated pupil.
- Nausea, vomiting, weakness.

Treatment/Care

Glaucoma may not be preventable, but the blindness that could result from it is. Ask to be tested for glaucoma whenever you get a regular vision checkup. It's a simple, painless procedure. If pressure inside the eyeball is high, an eye specialist (ophthalmologist) will probably give you eye drops and perhaps oral medicines. The aim of both is to reduce the pressure inside the eye.

Glaucoma, continued

Medicines given for acute glaucoma are prescribed for life. If you have glaucoma, let your doctor know or remind him or her of any medicines you take.

Also, do not take any medicine including over-the-counter ones without first checking with you doctor or pharmacist. Most cold medications and sleeping pills, for example, can cause the pupil in the eye to dilate. This can lead to increased eye pressure which is not recommended with glaucoma.

If medicines do not control the pressure, other options exist:

❑ Ultrasound which uses sound waves to reduce the pressure in the eye. This is usually done as a short, outpatient procedure.

❑ Laser beam surgery and other surgical procedures which can widen the drainage channels within the eye. These relieve fluid buildup.

There are also some things you can do on your own:

❑ Avoid getting upset and fatigued. They can increase pressure in the eye.

❑ Don't smoke cigarettes. It causes blood vessels to constrict which reduces blood supply to the eye.

11. High Blood Pressure

High blood pressure, (hypertension) isn't like a toothache, a bruise, or constipation. Nothing hurts, looks discolored, or fails to work. Usually, people with high blood pressure experience no discomfort or outward signs of trouble. Yet high blood pressure is a killer, a silent killer. Directly or indirectly, high blood pressure accounts for nearly a million deaths a year. Uncontrolled, high blood pressure increases the odds that you'll have a heart attack, a stroke, kidney failure or loss of vision.

High blood pressure happens when your blood moves through your arteries at a higher pressure than normal. The heart is actually straining to pump blood through the arteries. This isn't healthy because:

❑ It promotes hardening of the arteries (atherosclerosis). Hardened, narrowed, arteries may not be able to carry the amount of blood the body's organs and tissues need.

❑ Blood clots can form or lodge in a narrowed artery. This could cause a stroke or heart attack.

❑ The heart can become enlarged. This could result in congestive heart failure.

High Blood Pressure, continued

More than half of all older adults have high blood pressure. About fifty percent of all people who have it don't know it. Worse yet, many people who know their blood pressure is dangerously high are doing nothing to try to control it. And for 90 percent of those affected, there is no known cause. When this is the case, it is called primary or essential hypertension.

When high blood pressure results from another medical disorder or a medicine, it is referred to as secondary hypertension. In these cases, (about 10% of total), when the root cause is corrected, blood pressure usually goes back to normal.

Detection

How's your blood pressure? Blood pressure is normally measured with a blood pressure cuff placed on the arm. The numbers on the gauge measure your blood pressure in millimeters of mercury (mmHg). The first (higher) number measures the systolic pressure. This is the maximum pressure exerted against the arterial walls while the heart is beating. The second (lower) number records the diastolic pressure, the pressure between heart beats, when the heart is resting. The results are then recorded as systolic/diastolic pressure (120/80 mmHg, for example). Blood pressure is considered high in adults if it is consistently a reading of 140 mmHg systolic and/or 90 mmHg diastolic or higher.

To accurately determine your blood pressure, an average of two or more readings should be taken on two or more separate occasions. If your blood pressure is generally pretty good and suddenly registers high, don't be alarmed. Anxiety and other strong emotions, physical exertion, drinking a large amount of coffee, or digesting a recently consumed meal can temporarily elevate normal blood pressure with no lasting effects.

If, after several readings, your doctor is convinced you do indeed have high blood pressure, follow his or her advice. The risk of stroke, heart attack, and kidney disease increases when blood pressure is in the mild to moderate range.

Treatment and Care

The amazing part is, blood pressure is one of the easiest health problems to control. Here's a multi-point plan to control high blood pressure:

☐ If you're overweight, lose weight.

☐ Don't smoke.

☐ Limit alcohol to two drinks or less a day.

☐ Reduce your salt intake. This is helpful for many people. Use salt substitutes if your physician says it's okay.

☐ Keep caffeine intake to a minimum.

☐ Get regular exercise at least three times a week.

☐ Learn to handle stress by practicing relaxation techniques and rethinking stressful situations.

☐ Take any prescribed blood pressure medicine as directed. Don't skip your pills because you feel fine or because you don't like the side effects. Tell your doctor if you have any side effects of the medicine such as dizziness, faintness, skin rash, or even a dry cough in the absence of a cold. Another medicine can be prescribed.

☐ Talk to your physician or pharmacist before you take antihistamines and decongestants. Ingredients in some of these can raise your blood pressure.

☐ Don't eat black licorice.

12. Osteoporosis

Osteoporosis is a major health problem that affects more than 25 million Americans. Persons with osteoporosis suffer from a loss in bone mass and bone strength. Their bones become weak and brittle which makes them more prone to fracture. Any bone can be affected by osteoporosis, but the hips, wrists, and spine are the most common sites. Peak bone mass is reached between the ages of 25 and 35 years. After 35, everyone's bones lose density.

The actual causes of osteoporosis are unknown. Certain risk factors, however, increase the likelihood of developing osteoporosis:

☐ Being female - women are four times more likely to develop osteoporosis than men. The reasons are as follows:

• Their bones are generally thinner and lighter.

• They live longer than men.

• They have rapid bone loss at menopause due to a sharp decline of estrogen. The risk also increases for women who experience menopause before age 45 naturally or as a result of surgery which removes the ovaries and for women who experience a lack of or irregular menstrual flow.

☐ Having a thin, small framed body.

☐ Race - Caucasians and Asians are at a higher risk than blacks.

☐ Having red or blond hair or freckles may also increase the risk.

Osteoporosis, continued

- [ ] Lack of physical activity especially activities such as walking, running, tennis, and other weight-bearing exercises.

- [ ] Lack of calcium - adequate calcium intake throughout life helps to insure that calcium deficiency does not contribute to a weakening of bone mass.

- [ ] Heredity - the risk increases if there is a history of osteoporosis and/or bone fractures in your family.

- [ ] Cigarette smoking.

- [ ] Alcohol - regularly consuming alcoholic beverages, even as little as two to three ounces per day, may be damaging to bones.

- [ ] Heavy drinkers often have poor nutrition and may be more prone to fractures from their predisposition to falls.

- [ ] Taking certain medicines such as corticosteroids (anti-inflammatory medicines used to treat a variety of conditions such as asthma, arthritis, lupus, etc.) can lead to bone tissue loss. Some anti-seizure medicines and over-use of thyroid hormones may also increase the risk.

- [ ] Other disorders such as hyperthyroidism, hyperparathyroidism, and certain forms of bone cancer can also increase the risk.

Prevention

To prevent or slow osteoporosis, take these steps now:

- [ ] Be sure to eat a balanced diet including adequate daily intakes of calcium. The National Osteoporosis Foundation recommends 1000 milligrams a day for adults and 1500 milligrams a day for post-menopausal women not on estrogen replacement therapy, (ERT). The Recommended Dietary Allowance RDA is 800 milligrams a day.

To get your recommended calcium:

- [ ] Choose high calcium foods daily.

  - Skim and low-fat milks, yogurts, and cheeses *[Note: If you are lactose intolerant, you may need to use dairy products that are treated with the enzyme lactase or you can add this enzyme in over-the-counter drops or tablets.]*

  - Soft-boned fish and shellfish such as salmon, sardines.

  - Vegetables, especially broccoli, kale, collards.

  - Beans and bean sprouts as well as tofu (soy bean curd, if processed with calcium).

  - Calcium-fortified foods such as some orange juices, apple juices, ready to eat cereals, and breads.

Osteoporosis, continued

- [ ] Check with your doctor about taking calcium supplements if necessary.

- [ ] Follow a program of regular, weight-bearing exercise at least three or four times a week. Examples include walking, jogging, low-impact or non-impact aerobics.

- [ ] Do not smoke. Smoking makes osteoporosis worse and may negate the beneficial effects of estrogen replacement therapy (ERT).

- [ ] Limit alcohol consumption.

- [ ] Check with your doctor regarding medical management to prevent and treat osteoporosis especially if you are at a high risk of getting the disorder. He or she may prescribe estrogen replacement therapy (ERT), if you are female. This can prevent fractures from osteoporosis if started during or soon after menopause and taken for several years. There are risks with ERT, though, so you need to check with your doctor to see how they apply to you.

Signs and Symptoms

Osteoporosis is a "silent disease" because it can progress without any noticeable signs or symptoms. Often the first sign is when a bone fracture occurs. Symptoms include:

- [ ] A gradual loss of height.

- [ ] A rounding of the shoulders.

- [ ] Gum inflammation and loosening of the teeth.

- [ ] Acute lower backache.

- [ ] Swelling of a wrist after a fall.

Treatment and Care

Medical tests (absorptiometry, densitometry) can measure bone mass in various sites of the body. They are safe and painless. These tests can help doctors decide if and what kind of treatment is needed.

Treatment for osteoporosis includes:

- [ ] Dietary measures: A balanced diet rich in calcium and calcium supplementation if necessary.

- [ ] Daily exercises approved by your doctor.

- [ ] Fall prevention strategies:

  - Use grab bars and safety mats or non-skid tape on your tub or shower.

  - Use handrails on stairways.

  - Don't stoop to pick up things. Pick things up by bending your knees and keeping your back straight.

  - Wear flat, sturdy, non-skid shoes.

  - If you use throw rugs, make sure they have non-skid backs.

Osteoporosis, continued

- Use a cane or walker if necessary.
- See that halls, stairways and entrances are well lit. Use night lights in your bathroom, hallways, etc.

☐ Proper posture.

☐ Medications - two medicines have been approved by the Food & Drug Administration (FDA) to treat osteoporosis. They are estrogen replacement therapy (ERT) and calcitonin.

☐ Surgery (such as a hip replacement), if necessary.

13. Parkinson's Disease

Parkinson's disease is a nervous system disorder. It causes tremors in which there is involuntary shaking in the limbs and head, a shuffling gait, and stiffness. With it comes a gradual, progressive stiffness of muscles. Parkinson's disease is one that is common only in older adults.

It most often strikes people over 60 years of age. The cause of Parkinson's disease is not known. It results from the degeneration of cells in the part of the brain that produces dopamine, a substance nerves need to function properly.

Signs and Symptoms

The signs and symptoms of Parkinson's disease include:

☐ Slow or stiff movement.

☐ Stooped posture.

☐ Shuffling or dragging of the feet.

☐ Tremors and shaking of the head.

☐ Monotone voice, weak and high-pitched.

☐ Blinking less frequently than normal.

☐ Lack of spontaneity in facial expression.

☐ Problems in swallowing.

☐ Difficulty in adjusting positions.

☐ Depression and anxiety.

☐ Dementia (in advanced stages).

Treatment and Care

Parkinson's disease is not yet curable. Great strides have been made in treatment, offering new hope for the nearly one million middle-aged and older people who are affected. For the most part, symptoms can be relieved or controlled. Parkinson's disease does not significantly lower life expectancy.

Medications such as Levodopa and Sinemet increase the dopamine level in the brain. For many people, these medicines control symptoms. Another medicine, Eldepryl, is sometimes used with Levodopa or Carbidopa to enhance their effects and may help to slow the progression of the disease.

Parkinson's Disease, continued

Other treatments try to make the person with Parkinson's more comfortable. Warm baths and massages, for example, can help prevent muscle rigidity. Here are some other helpful hints:

- ☐ Take care to maintain a safe home environment. For example, replace razor blades with electric shavers, use non-skid rugs, handrails etc., to prevent falls.

- ☐ Simplify tasks. (Replace tie shoes with loafers, for instance, or wear clothing that can be pulled on or that have zippers or velcro closures instead of buttons.

- ☐ Include high-fiber foods in the diet and drink lots of fluids, to prevent constipation.

- ☐ Get expert physical therapy.

- ☐ Remain as active as possible.

- ☐ Get professional help to relieve depression, if necessary.

14. Pneumonia

Despite medical advances, including the use of antibiotics, pneumonia is still the sixth leading cause of death in the United States.

Pneumonia can develop when the lungs are infected by either bacteria, viruses, fungi, or toxins causing inflammation. Certain people are at a greater risk for pneumonia than others. They include:

- ☐ Elderly people, because the body's ability to fight off disease diminishes with age.

- ☐ People who are hospitalized for other conditions.

- ☐ Individuals with suppressed cough reflex following a stroke.

- ☐ Smokers, because tobacco smoke paralyzes the tiny hairs that otherwise help to expel germ-ridden mucus from the lungs.

- ☐ People who suffer from malnutrition, alcoholism, or viral infections.

- ☐ Anyone with a recent respiratory viral infection.

- ☐ People with emphysema or chronic bronchitis.

- ☐ People with sickle cell anemia.

- ☐ Cancer patients undergoing radiation treatments or chemotherapy, both of which wear down the immune system.

- ☐ People with AIDS (acquired immune deficiency syndrome - HIV (human immune deficiency virus).

Pneumonia, continued

Signs and Symptoms

Pneumonia symptoms include:

- ☐ Chest pain (may worsen when inhaling).
- ☐ Fever and chills.
- ☐ Coughing with little or no sputum or sometimes with bloody, dark yellow or rust-colored sputum.
- ☐ Difficulty in breathing, rapid breathing.
- ☐ General fatigue, headache, nausea, vomiting.
- ☐ Bluish lips and fingertips.

Treatment/Care/Prevention

Treatment for pneumonia will depend on its type (viral, bacterial or chemical, for example) and location. X-rays and sputum analysis and blood tests can help identify these.

Treatment includes:

- ☐ Getting plenty of bed rest.
- ☐ Using a cool-mist humidifier in the room or rooms in which you spend the bulk of your time.
- ☐ Drinking plenty of fluids.
- ☐ Taking acetaminophen to relieve minor discomfort and reduce fever.
- ☐ Taking any medications your doctor prescribes. Antibiotics are used to treat bacterial pneumonia or to fight a secondary bacterial infection. Nose drops, sprays or oral decongestants to treat congestion in the upper respiratory tract.
- ☐ Cough medicines as needed, a cough suppressant for a dry, non-productive cough, an expectorant type for a mucus producing cough.
- ☐ Oxygen therapy if you are breathless and turning blue.
- ☐ Removing fluid from the lungs by suction, anti-inflammatory medicines, and oxygen therapy may be used for chemically induced pneumonias.
- ☐ Also, vaccines against influenza and pneumonococcus (pneumonia bacteria) are available. They are recommended in elderly persons and others with chronic diseases. Ask your doctor about them.

15. Strokes

Strokes (also called cerebrovascular accidents, or apoplexy) are the third leading cause of death in the United States. A stroke can be caused by lack of blood and therefore lack of oxygen to the brain, usually due to either clogged arteries or rupture of a blood vessel in the brain. In either case, the

Strokes, continued

ther case, the end result is brain damage (and possible death). Persons who suffer from both high blood pressure and hardening of the arteries are most susceptible to having a stroke. A stroke can happen suddenly, but it often follows years of the slow buildup of fatty deposits inside the blood vessels.

Some people experience a temporary "mini-stroke", or a transient ischemic attack (TIA). The symptoms mimic a stroke, (see below) but clear within 24 hours. TIAs are a warning that a real stroke may follow.

Prevention

Measures can be taken to prevent a stroke. Here's what to do to reduce the risks of a stroke:

- ☐ Control your blood pressure. Have it checked regularly and, if necessary, take medication prescribed by your physician.
- ☐ Reduce blood levels of cholesterol to below 200 milligrams per deciliter (measured by a blood test).
- ☐ Get regular exercise.
- ☐ Keep your weight down.
- ☐ Don't smoke.
- ☐ Keep blood sugar levels under control if you're diabetic.
- ☐ Use alcohol in moderation, if at all.
- ☐ Learn to manage stress.
- ☐ Ask your doctor about taking aspirin (low-dose, such as a daily baby aspirin). Some studies show

this may help prevent strokes.

Signs and Symptoms

It's important to know the warning signals of a stroke and get immediate medical attention, to minimize the damage. To help you remember what to look out for, the initials of the signs and symptoms spell DANGER.

- ☐ **D**izziness.
- ☐ **A**bsent-mindedness, or temporary loss of memory or mental ability.
- ☐ **N**umbness or weakness in the face, arm, or leg.
- ☐ **G**arbled speech.
- ☐ **E**ye problems, including temporary loss of sight in one eye, or double vision.
- ☐ **R**ecent onset of severe headaches.

Care and Treatment

Tests can be done to locate the obstruction of blood flow to the brain. The doctor may then prescribe appropriate medicines and/or surgery.

When an actual stroke occurs, it is crucial to get immediate treatment. Treatment includes:

- ☐ Medicines that reduce brain tissue swelling, control blood pressure, and inhibit the normal clotting of the blood or prevent existing clots from getting bigger.
- ☐ Surgery if warranted.
- ☐ Rehabilitation as needed by speech, physical, and occupational therapists.

Appendices

Appendix A

Calling Your Doctor Checklist

Sometimes you need to call your doctor. Get the answers to these questions before that time comes:

- [ ] What is the best time to call?

- [ ] What is the doctor's rule for returning calls?

- [ ] Who should you talk to if the doctor can't come to the phone?

- [ ] What is the phone number for emergency calls or calls when the office is closed?

- [ ] Who do you call if your doctor is out of town?

When you reach your doctor by phone:

- [ ] Get to the point of your call quickly, especially if you've phoned the doctor after office hours. (Have someone else call the doctor for you if you can't do it yourself).

- [ ] Tell your symptoms and problems. Write them down and keep them by the telephone so you don't have to remember them.

- [ ] Report results of home tests and things you have been keeping track of. Here are some examples: Temperature of 101°F for 2 days, diarrhea that has lasted 48 hours, etc.

- [ ] Ask the doctor what to do. Write it down.

- [ ] Have your pharmacist's phone number handy in case the doctor needs to prescribe medicine.

- [ ] Ask the doctor if you should call him or her back, or if you should come to the office.

- [ ] Ask the doctor if you should go to the emergency room. He or she may tell you to go only if you get other symptoms. Write down the symptoms to watch for.

- [ ] Thank the doctor for talking to you on the telephone.

Appendix B

Visiting Your Doctor Checklist

It's easy to forget to ask your doctor all your questions. The checklist below lists what things you should find out. You may want to copy the list and take it with you.

Diagnosis (What's wrong?)

- [ ] Is there a simple reason for my problem? Ask the doctor to explain any medical terms you don't know.

Visiting Your Doctor
Checklist, continued

☐ Do I need more testing? If so, what? How much do these tests cost? Will my insurance cover them? Where do I get the information?

Prognosis (What will happen?)

☐ How will this problem affect me in the future?

Treatment (What should I do?)

☐ What treatment should I follow? (This could include medical treatment, or changes in diet or lifestyle.)

☐ What will happen if I don't treat it now?

☐ How do I get ready for any tests that I need?

☐ Do I call to schedule the test or does your office do it for me?

☐ When and how will I get the test results?

☐ Should I call you?

☐ When do you want to see me again?

☐ What else should I know?

☐ Can I get any more information about this problem?

☐ Are there any local or national health organizations that I could call or write to for more information? Do you have their numbers and/or addresses?

☐ Where should I go if I need emergency care?

Specialists (What about seeing another doctor?)

☐ Should I see a specialist? If yes, who should I see? Can you write this down for me?

☐ Does this specialist work out of more than one office?

☐ Is this person board certified?

☐ How soon should I be seen by this specialist?

☐ What if I can't get an appointment for a month or more? Can you help me get in sooner, or should I try to see someone else?

Surgery (What if I need an operation?)

☐ Do I need surgery at this time?

☐ Do I have any choices *instead* of surgery?

☐ What are the risks?

☐ Where will I have this surgery?

☐ Can I have the surgery as an outpatient?

☐ What will the surgery and follow up care cost? What will my insurance pay?

Visiting Your Doctor Checklist, continued

- ☐ Who will do the surgery? How many times has this surgeon done this procedure?

- ☐ Where can I get a second opinion? Know if your insurance company needs a second opinion for surgery. Find out what their rules are. Your insurance company may want you to call a certain number and use certain doctors for second opinions.

Doctor Fees (How much will this cost me?)

- ☐ What will this office visit cost me today?

- ☐ What will the fees for other services be? Ask this before you get the services.

- ☐ What does my health insurance cover?

Appendix C

Medications Checklist

Questions you should ask when given a prescription include:

- ☐ What will medication do for me?

- ☐ What is the name of the medicine?

- ☐ Is there a generic one? Is it equally effective?

- ☐ How and when should I take it?

- ☐ Are there any foods, drinks or things I should avoid when I take this medicine? (Examples: Alcohol, other medicine and/or sunlight)?

- ☐ What should I do if I forget to take it?

- ☐ Should I expect side effects?

- ☐ If I feel better should I stop using it?

- ☐ Will I have to take this medicine for a short time or from now on?

- ☐ Will this medicine be OK to take with medicines I am already taking?

- ☐ Tell the doctor every medication you take when you get a prescription. Use the Medication Log on page 124 to keep track. Have it with you when you talk to the doctor.

D. Medication Log
(Photocopy as needed)

	Medicine Name and Dose	Reason for Taking	Prescribing Doctor	Date Started/ Stopped	Notes/Side Effects
1.					
2.					
3.					
4.					
5.					
6.					
7.					
8.					
9.					
10.					

Appendix E Medical Records

Disease History

(Fill in dates for each one, if applicable)

Name	Chicken Pox	Whooping Cough	Meningitis	Hepatitis	Tuberculosis	Scarlet Fever	Mononucleosis	Pneumonia	Other (List)
1.									
2.									
3.									
4.									
5.									

Health Information

Name	Blood Type	Rh (+ / -)	Drug Sensitivities	Allergies
1.				
2.				
3.				
4.				
5.				

Illness / Hospital Records

Name	Illness, Injury/Surgery	Date(s)	Method of Treatment	Doctor/Hospital	Comments
1.					
2.					
3.					
4.					
5.					

Appendix F

Your Home Pharmacy

Below is a list of some over-the-counter (OTC) medications and supplies that you may need for self-care.

☐ Ask your doctor which OTC products are safe for you to use and when you should use them.

☐ Read warning sections on labels. These list the conditions under which the medicine should not be taken.

☐ Ask if you should follow the instructions on the labels or take in a different way.

☐ Check the expiration dates. Discard ones that have expired. Replace items as needed.

Medications	Use(s)
1. Acetaminophen ex: Aspirin-Free Anacin, Tylenol	Pain relief, reduces fever
2. Activated charcoal (binds certain chemicals when swallowed) [Note: Call Poison Control Center first]	Oral Poisoning, for some poisons
3. Antacids (liquid or tablets) ex: Tums, Rolaids, Mylanta, Amphojel, Riopan	Stomach upset, heartburn
4. Antibiotic cream or ointment ex: Neosporin	Minor skin infection, wounds
5. Anti-diarrheal medicine ex: Kaopectate, Immodium A-D, Donnagel	Diarrhea
6. Antifungal preparations ex: Tinactin	Fungal infections such as athlete's foot
7. Antihistamines ex: Dristan, Triaminic, Benadryl	Allergies, cold symptom relief
8. Anti-motion sickness ex: Dramamine	Motion sickness
9. Antiseptic preparation ex: Betadine	Abrasions, cuts
10. Aspirin ex: Anacin, Bayer, Bufferin	Pain relief, reduces fever and swelling
11. Cough medicine with expectorant (look for one with Guaifenesin) ex: Robitussin	Cough with mucus

Your Home Pharmacy, continued

Medications	Use(s)
12. Cough suppressant without expectorant (look for one with Dextromethorphan ex: Robitussin DM	Dry cough without mucus
13. Decongestant (tablets, nose spray, etc.) ex: Dristan Nasal Spray, Sudafed, Dimetapp	Stuffy and runny nose, post-nasal drip from colds, allergies
14. Ear wax dissolver ex: Audiologists Choice, Debrox	Ear wax
15. Eye drops and artificial tears ex: Murine, Visine	Minor eye irritations
16. Hemorrhoid preparations ex: Preparation H	Hemorrhoids
17. Hydrocortisone cream ex: Cortaid, Lanacort	Minor skin irritations, itching and rashes
18. Ibuprofen ex: Advil, Motrin	Pain relief, reduces fever and swelling
19. Laxatives ex: Ex-Lax, Correctol, Milk of Magnesia	Constipation
20. Naproxen Sodium ex: Aleve	Pain relief, reduces fever and swelling
21. Petroleum jelly ex: Vaseline	Chafing, dry skin
22. Rubbing alcohol	Topical antiseptic, clean thermometer
23. Stool Softeners ex: Colace Bulking agents ex: Metamucil	Prevent constipation
24. Sunscreen - look for one with SPF (sun protection factor) of 15 or more	Prevent sunburn, protect against skin cancer
25. Syrup of Ipecac (Note: Call Poison Control Center first)	To induce vomiting for some poisons
26. Throat anesthetic preparations ex: Sucret throat lozenges, Chloraseptic spray	Minor sore throat
27. Toothache relief preparation ex. Anbesol	Toothache

Home Pharmacy,
continued

Supplies	Use(s)
1. Adhesive bandages	Minor wounds
2. Adhesive tape, sterile gauze pads, roll of sterile gauze and scissors	To dress minor wounds
3. Cotton balls, cotton tipped applicators	To apply antiseptics etc. to minor wounds
4. Elastic bandages and clips	Minor strains and sprains
5. Heating pad/hot water bottle	Minor pains, strains
6. Humidifier, vaporizer (cool mist)	Add moisture to the air
7. Ice pack/Heat pack	Minor pain and injuries
8. Medicine Spoon	To measure right dose of liquid medicine
9. Moisturizer ex: Jergens lotion	Dry Skin
10. Thermometer (mercury-containing, digital, etc.)	Fever
11. Tongue depressor, flashlight	Check for redness or infection in throat
12. Tweezers	Remove splinters

For Special Needs and Ongoing Health Conditions

Supplies	Use(s)
1. Blood pressure cuff and stethoscope or self-measuring blood pressure kit	Measure blood pressure
2. Blood sugar test kit	Monitor blood sugar
3. Urine test strips (many types)	Measure for sugar in the urine or for urinary tract infection (Biotel UTI)